Meditating Selflessly

The MIT Press
Cambridge, Massachusetts
London, England

Meditating Selflessly

Practical Neural Zen

James H. Austin, M.D.

For information about special quantity discounts, please email special _sales@mitpress.mit.edu

This book was set in Palatino and Frutiger on InDesign by Asco Typesetters, Hong Kong.
Printed and bound in the United States of America.

Library of Congress Cataloging-in-Publication Data

Austin, James H., 1925–
Meditating selflessly : practical neural Zen / James H. Austin.
    p.   cm.
Includes bibliographical references and index.
ISBN 978-0-262-01587-5 (hardcover : alk. paper) 1. Meditation—Zen Buddhism—Miscellanea. 2. Zen Buddhism—Psychology—Miscellanea. 3. Self-consciousness (Awareness)—Religious aspects—Zen Buddhism—Miscellanea. I. Title.

BQ9288.A94   2011
294.3′4435—dc22   2010049673

10   9   8   7   6   5   4   3   2   1

To my early teachers Nanrei Kobori-Roshi, Myokyo-ni, and Joshu Sasaki-Roshi for their inspiration and to all those whose countless contributions to Zen, and to the brain sciences, are reviewed in these pages.

Getting free of the conceit that 'I am' — this is truly the greatest happiness of all.

The Buddha
(Udana 2:11; Pali Canon)

Contents in Brief

Contents in Detail

List of Figures

List of Tables

Preface

The most important thing is not to be self-centered.
                                        Zen Master Bankei (1622–1693)[1]

This is one more book of words about Zen. It is not your usual kind of "Self-help" book. Its major theme heeds Bankei's advice to be *less* Self-centered. The final paragraph of the previous book advised you to drop all intellectual concepts that you might have developed from its earlier pages. Instead, where were you invited to turn? Toward that open awareness awaiting you on the cushion and the mat. Because Zen isn't what *you* think *it* is. It's what is revealed *when you learn to let go of your intricate thinking Self.*[2]

This book begins where that paragraph left off. Its title suggests how to redirect such a quest toward a more open awareness. *Meditating Selflessly* goes on to explore particular ways to practice. Most of its suggestions are addressed to readers who are already meditating or who might consider meditating in the future. Why is *practical* in the subtitle? Because these pages explore commonsense, empirical prescriptions. They're intended to help meditators avoid endlessly reinforcing dysfunctional egocentricities.

Why neural? Neural acknowledges the term *neural Buddhism.* David Brooks coined this phrase in his *New York Times* article back in 2008.[3] Brooks was aware of the new wave of neuroscience research. He foresaw that it would go on to have significant cultural effects. Contributing to this research were "scientists whose beliefs overlap a bit with Buddhism." This slender volume reflects only one small part of this new wave as it appears to one academic neurologist. The word *Zen* also occurs next in the subtitle because the author has practiced in the tradition of this Buddhist school for some 37 years.

Today's spiritual supermarket offers many diverse styles of meditation. They are represented by teachers who describe their particular techniques in detail. This book comes from a different direction. While it often discusses useful methods ascribed to the Buddha, it highlights only particular techniques that seem practical when viewed through the lens of the latest *neural*-Zen perspective. Accordingly, these new proposals often reflect the covert ways that our normal brain's attention networks have recently been found to open up and process that vast other reality lying beyond the immediate grasp of our own egocentric Self.

Are such suggestions valid? Readers who wish to know more can consult selected samples of the most recent and most ancient research in the sections labeled "background." For your convenience, further information on many topics discussed here is also cross-referenced [using brackets] to pages in three earlier books. For example, you'll discover *Zen and the Brain* abbreviated in the text as [ZB: __]. *Zen-Brain Reflections* is [ZBR: __]. *Selfless Insight* is [SI: __].

A series of "do's" and "don'ts" is scattered throughout the book. You can recognize each "*do*" because it is preceded by a bullet (•). The few "*don'ts*" in the text refer to disadvantageous attitudes or behaviors that might have negative consequences. They are preceded by an asterisk (*).

A section at the end of the book collects all these *do's* and *don'ts* for a quick review. Both types of entries—• and *—are presented as empirical suggestions. None is carved in stone. If a meditator were to view them as some kind of prescription, there always remains plenty of room for individual adjustments, including noncompliance.

- **Practicing doesn't mean you're obsessed with having to achieve perfection. Practice just means you're not perfect.**

On these pages, practice also means that we'll be going beyond mere Self-conscious thoughts and concepts to emphasize the benefits of actual repeated direct experience. Repetition is the operative word.

.

Acknowledgments

I'm indebted to Phillip Laughlin at MIT Press for appreciating the need to bring this slender volume to the attention of the wider meditating and neuroscience communities. Again, my thanks go to Katherine Arnoldi Almeida for her skilled editorial assistance and to Yasuyo Iguchi for her artistic skill in designing the cover and icons.

I'm especially grateful to Lauren Elliott for her ongoing patience in deciphering my handwriting on multiple drafts of her excellent typing, and for helping to keep this manuscript organized as it expanded. Many thanks go also to James W. Austin, Scott W. Austin, Seido Ray Ronci, and Janice Gaston for their valued assistance in reviewing and commenting on the manuscript. I also thank Scott Greathouse and Adam Newman for their skill in bringing the figures to fruition, and my calligraphy teacher, Tanchu Terayama, for the generous parting gift of his original calligraphy that included the *mu* (emptiness) character illustrated on the jacket cover.

In recent years, I have been privileged to share in the inestimable bounties of regular Zen practice with our sangha at Hokoku-an led by Seido Ray Ronci, in the activities of Show-Me Dharma, led by Virginia Morgan, and in those of the Dancing Crane Zen Center, led by Meredith Garmon. Gassho to all!

This book manuscript was prepared for MIT Press in 2010, shortly before a short manuscript was due for another publication, which accounts for some inevitable overlappings in their respective topics and contents. Accordingly, grateful credit is acknowledged to (1) Springer Science and Business Media for the inclusion of certain material from the chapter entitled The meditative approach to awaken selfless insight-wisdom, in S. Schmidt and H. Walach (Eds.) *Neuroscience, Consciousness and Spirituality*, Springer, 2012, in press.

By Way of a Personal Introduction

> The psyche is distinctly more complicated and inaccessible than the body.
>
> Carl Jung (1875–1961)

I began the Zen training of my psyche and soma late. It began during a research sabbatical in Kyoto in 1974, when I was fortunate to meet an English-speaking Zen master. Nanrei Kobori-Roshi enabled me to begin Zen practice at Daitoku-ji, a Rinzai Zen temple.[1] Later in my practice there, while meditating one evening, my *physical* sense of Self vanished as I dropped into a state of deep internal absorption. During a second sabbatical from 1981 to 1982, I was privileged to continue Zen training with Myokyo-ni at the Zen Centre in London. En route to the second day of a retreat, as I happened to gaze casually off into the sky, my entire *psychic* sense of Self dissolved into a state of *kensho*.

How had meditative practices enabled these states to change my psyche and soma? In no way had any prior training as an academic neurologist prepared me to understand either experience. A period of reeducation began.[2-8]

Throughout the course of this research, these brief phenomena had already made one thing clear: they had involved *subtractions* of the Self. The sense of my body (my *somatic* Self) had been the first to drop off. Only years later had the Self of the *psyche* vanished briefly. The two subtractions of the Self were completely different. Different sets of inhibitory events seemed to have converged in the brain during each state. But how? It was plausible to relate most inhibitory events to the level of the thalamus, our gateway to consciousness far down in the center of the brain [ZB: 589–592].

By the time of the Mind and Life Summer Research Institute meeting in June 2006, substantial neuroimaging evidence had finally become available in ways that could support the model of a novel thalamic hypothesis for kensho. By then, position emission tomography (PET) and functional magnetic resonance imaging (fMRI) data had indicated which networks on the *outside* surface of the brain were serving our normal functions of attention. Moreover, these networks displayed more than an inherent capacity to react by shifting their activities up or down. Indeed, when they shifted, it would be into *reciprocal, seesaw relationships* with key regions chiefly on the *inside* surface of the brain.

Many of our more personalized functions were represented here, along the midline. Their networks expressed both the layered constructs of our psychic Self and its interactions with the details of the outside environment.[9,10] Zen had emphasized attention for centuries. Finally, it seemed that attention was turning out to have a pivotal role for meditators. At least in the fMRI data, attention regions correlated *inversely* with the regions related more to the Self.

Researchers had begun to evolve two other related sets of major distinctions during the first decade of this new century. One important set would distinguish between *top-down* attention and *bottom-up* attention. The second set would distinguish between *Self-referential* processing and *other-referential* processing. In this instance, "other" meant things in the other world outside us. Notably, the pairings in each category of brain function are to be viewed as *complementary*, not antagonistic. Indeed, they are almost like yin and yang. At the end of this book, a closing summary explains how these topics unfold in sequences. In the model proposed for kensho, these conceptual steps help clarify the ancient paradox: selflessness and insight-wisdom *co-arise* simultaneously.

Do we now know every fine detail of the signals that enable the attention networks to process various assigned tasks *and* to simultaneously diminish the Self? No. These are among the many key research issues awaiting further refinement.[11,12,13] Meanwhile, it seemed important to alert the meditating and neuroscientist communities to some practical implications of the information already available. And so these pages invite you to test these preliminary suggestions and to determine whether their basic principles are applicable to where *you* are right now on your own long-term path of meditative training.

No suggestions made here belong to any single spiritual tradition, doctrine, school, or system of philosophical belief. Instead, what you may glimpse are some of your brain's innate resources. These draw upon evolution's hard-won neural pathways that ensured survival. They tap into implicit instinctual capacities and the kinds of native intelligence that are of universal neurobiological importance. Nothing unique is proposed here. Some of it used to be called "horse sense."[14]

Readers had commented favorably on the short question-and-answer (*mondo*) chapters that summarized complex topics in each of the earlier Zen books. This volume expands this custom, inserting questions and answers frequently throughout the text. The next paragraphs provide a brief example of this simplified approach. They return to part of an interview conducted early in 2009.

You've spent decades studying the relationships between Zen and the brain. What's changed during these years?

A new field of meditative neuroscience has opened up. It shares contributions from both brain-based research and Buddhist scholarship. In the course of observing this major trend, my own understanding of Zen has gradually evolved. Also, as a practitioner, I've become aware of how many of my earlier, hard-edged, overconditioned responses seem to have been "rounded off," as it were.

Is studying the brain of a meditating person now a legitimate field of scientific research?

Yes. For millennia, diverse spiritual traditions have attested to the "fruits of meditation." It's reasonable to inquire whether objective findings support such alleged practical benefits. But research is worthwhile for another reason: we learn much more about the normal functions of both our brain *and* our body as soon as we seek to clarify how meditative training transforms consciousness.

Can learning how to meditate help me improve my everyday personal performance skills and interpersonal relationships?

Meditation is an attentive art. When we train our attentive capacities through regular meditative practices, we begin to develop enhanced degrees of emotional clarity and stability. These in turn help us to identify our own emotions and to realize how we can modify our behavioral responses in ways that are more adaptive.

Moreover, meditation is increasingly linked with a variety of health benefits. Examples include an improved ability to relax, lower blood pressure, and enhanced antibody responses to an influenza vaccination.

Part I

An Introduction to Selfless Meditation

In all that you do, be even and balanced and attuned
to the inherent equality of all things—becoming selfless and without attachments.

Ch'an Master Yuan-wu Kequin (1063–1135)

1

What Is Meditation? What Is Zen?

> Taste as much of this as you can. Swallow what you need, and
> spit out the rest.
>> Zen Master Taizan Maezumi (1931–1995)[1]
> (Advice to his disciples, with regard to importing Asian teach-
> ings into the West.)

> The fact that you are a Zen Buddhist and I am a Christian
> monk, far from separating us, makes us most like one another.
> How many centuries is it going to take for people to discover
> this fact . . . ?
>> Thomas Merton (1915–1968)[2]
>> (Letter to D. T. Suzuki)

What Is Meditation?

You might begin to think of meditation as a refreshing pause.
In solitude, we gradually begin to realize a simple fact:
we've become emotionally attached to ideas about people
and things. Indeed, we're hooked in ways—pro and con—
that cause huge problems in our daily life.

*The mythologies of Western and Middle-Eastern religions are
already too much for me. Why should I be interested in any alien
belief systems imported from Asia?*

- **Find some assurance in the evidence: meditation
  has been tested and found useful for millennia by
  many cultures and spiritual traditions.**
  When conservative meditative practices are repeated
  on a regular daily basis, it is generally agreed that
  they offer a remedy for many sufferings that arise in
  your overconditioned Self. Please note that the word

Self begins with a capital S in these pages. This is simply to indicate that the source for many of our biggest personal problems lies in the way the Self has been overconditioned [ZB: 327–334].

Much recent evidence can also be interpreted to support a further belief: authentic, long-term meditative training has the potential to slowly transform many unfruitful character traits toward more wholesome, affirmative directions [ZB: 625–697; ZBR: 388–401; SI: 173–178, 207–215, 223–244].

What Is Zen? Why Is Zen so Identified with Meditation?

Zen is a pragmatic school of Mahayana Buddhism. It is viewed here as an inspired human product. Its basic belief system and practices celebrate the lightning strike of creative insight that awakened its founder. They further emphasize that a program of deep meditative training—not just superficial intellectual learning—precedes such an insight. This long Path of mindful, introspective training enables meditators to live more selflessly, and with increasing compassion, in each present moment of *this* world—as *it really is*—not as they prefer to think, hope, and believe it "ought" to be.

Embedded in the very word *Zen* is the story of how its emphasis on meditation evolved over the centuries. The origin of the word can be traced back to the ancient practices of Yoga in an era when the old Sanskrit term for meditation was *dhyana*. Then, around 563 B.C.E., an exemplary man was born in what is now southern Nepal. After six rigorous years of practice, Siddhartha became enlightened while meditating under the Bodhi tree. It was for this reason that he would eventually be called the Buddha, meaning the Awakened One.

Centuries later, Buddhist monks spread his enlightened teachings north from the Indian subcontinent into China. Here they were assimilated into the established Chinese cultures of Taoism and Confucianism. In Chinese, the old word *dhyana* evolved into *Ch'an*. When this blended form of Buddhist meditation reached Japan during the twelfth and thirteenth centuries, *Zen* became the way the Japanese pronounced Ch'an. The term *zazen* refers to its system of meditation.

The ideogram for Zen includes two components. One is the character *shi* (to show). The other is the character for *tan* (single). They can be interpreted in a way that hints at the ultimate refinement of perception: a state of consciousness capable of revealing all reality as characterized by *One* "singleness of mind," not by the split into our usual Self/other duality.[3] The major Zen Buddhist schools are the Rinzai and Soto schools [ZB: 7–11].

The writings of D. T. Suzuki brought Zen increasingly to the West's attention after World War II. Ideas about the psychological and sociological aspects of Zen have gone on to expand exponentially since then. Not only has attention per se become a field of research that can attract more than two thousand articles each year, but investigators have finally begun to pursue the interactive circuitries of our omni-Self into diverse networks of the brain. The next four chapters examine how these latest trends of research into attention intersect with research trying to understand the elusive nature of the Self. Throughout the book as a whole will run the same theme advocated by Master Yuan-wu back in the epigram that opens part I.

- **"Be even and balanced" in your attentiveness, becoming "attuned to the inherent equality of all things."**

2

Attentiveness and the Self

> Time flies like an arrow, so be careful not to waste energy on trivial matters. Be attentive! Be attentive!
>
> Zen Master Daito Kokushi (1283–1337)

> In Buddhism, the ego is the main culprit. It insists on setting itself up against others, creating barriers and obstacles, oppositions and contradictions.
>
> Nanrei Kobori-Roshi (1918–1992)

Daito Kokushi founded Daitoku-ji monastery. Six centuries later, my teacher Kobori-Roshi would walk on the same temple grounds and serve for a while as its abbot. Both understood the two themes central to Zen training: attention and the Self.

Why are Zen teachings so explicit, both about the training of attention and the problems caused by our egocentric Self?

Zen follows an age-old, twofold approach. It happens to work for empirical reasons. It turns out that the long-term practice of training attention becomes an integral part of dissolving our over-conditioned Self. That's the main reason why this book frames the training of attentiveness in the context of our becoming *less* Self-centered.

Only during this decade has neuroimaging research shown that attention and Self—seemingly joined at the hip like twins—still represent functions that can pull in opposite directions. In fact, when we normally shift attention toward the external world, what effect does this shift have on our ever-dominant Self-centeredness? It usually diminishes it in an almost *reciprocal, seesaw* manner [ZBR: 193–218; SI: 109–117, 191–196].

In order to introduce the general notion of this *inverse* relationship between external attention and egocentricity, one might tentatively oversimply it visually as follows:

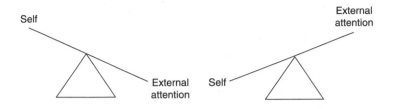

You might think these simple diagrams are counterintuitive and that they don't really apply to you. If so, it might help to take time out to recall two separate occasions. In one, you became so Self-absorbed inside your own internalized thoughts that your awareness of the outside world faded (as suggested in the left diagram). In the other, conversely, perhaps you recall some other relevant occasion similar to the one I remember. With me, it was the time when I became so absorbed in paying attention to the dramatic events on a movie screen that I didn't realize my leg had fallen asleep (as suggested in the diagram on the right.)

Maybe you're already wondering: Does any simple, logical connection exist between being self*less* and becoming "enlightened"? Well, some underlying steps do seem logical. However, they proceed through at least nine intermediate sequences, in the course of which pairs of opposing functions continue to unfold. No topics involved in these later steps are simple. (If you're interested in seeing where we'll be going with this model, the closing summary of this volume outlines their mechanisms.)

Is this kind of attentiveness the same as mindfulness?

When you're mindful, your attentive processing turns *nonjudgmentally* toward what is going on right at the *present moment*.

At this instant, you become acutely aware of *Just This, right NOW*. Perhaps the stimulus arrives from the sound of a bell or from some other external event occurring out there in the environment. Alternatively, you could be noticing internal sensations that are arising within your own body. Or you could be noticing your own feelings and thoughts. After a while, you'll recognize something so obvious that we tend to forget how crucial it is: all such events are *transitory*. They come and go [SI: 8–11]. They are temporary brain states. They are impermanent. You and I are also impermanent, although it takes decades for all of our attitudes to comprehend this sobering fact and adjust to it.

Well, does this kind of mindfulness also involve concentration?

It can. To concentrate means to amplify one's available powers of attention—*which includes attention's inherent links with mental processing*—while focusing these two coactive components toward a single common objective. Consider what usually happens when we first sit down to meditate. For example, a conventional way to begin to start concentrating is to *narrow* our focus of attention. We choose to unify it on one central spot that is usually down in front of us. Suppose, however, that we pause to analyze the ways we actually *feel* and *act* during each of the several different times that we concentrate. Then, we discover some variations on this theme of concentration.

1. We find that it's easier to concentrate when our baseline level of *arousal* is higher. Often this refers to the morning hours when we first feel wide awake. Kobori-Roshi taught me that "Early morning sitting is golden. Evening sitting is silver." It's much harder to concentrate when we're sleepy after a full meal or are overtired at night [ZB: 338–347].

2. We can deliberately vary the amplitude of the effort we put into concentrating. We can *fully exert* its power over a range from minimal to intense.

3. To accomplish any task, we must *sustain* the several mental and physical components involved in concentration. How long we can maintain this span of attention? To continue to focus for a long time at this requisite level of concentration is an art. With repeated practice the attention span grows longer.

4. Two prominent by-products are linked to both this *regular practice* of *concentrating our attention and* to the *co-enhanced processing capacities* that necessarily accompany it.

   a. Various distractions become less distracting;

   b. It becomes easier to realize, analyze, and actualize brief intuitions and insights of various sizes. Why? One reason is because we can now hold them on line for a longer period after they dart in.

5. Sometimes, a cycle of emotional arousal happens to surface in a particular setting. Then, attention concentrates with great intensity on a narrowly focused target. This automatic shift drops you into a one-pointed, usually brief state of meditative absorption [ZB: 467–479].

Background: Introduction to "Mindfulness," to the Limitations of Mere Words, and to the Question: Can I Stay Mindful Even when I'm Not Sitting and Meditating?

The Buddhist practice of mindfulness was described in the Buddha's Satipatthana Sutra. Mahasi Sayadaw[1] and Bikkhu Bodhi[2] are among the several Theravada monks of long experience who have discussed important points in this classic text. Its preliminary steps deserve repetition.

• **Commit yourself to start simplifying your lifestyle. This is no token gesture toward letting go. It means that with disciplined restraint, you have** finally decided to renounce particular longings and loathings identified as inappropriate. A more formal program of training can begin at this point.

· Note that you don't wall yourself off from experiencing life's vicissitudes. You still go on perceiving events in the real world.

As Zen Master Shunryu Suzuki said about impermanence, "Renunciation is not giving up the things of this world, but accepting that they go away" [ZB: 73–74]. Once you identify each unwholesome emotion, you can finally experience the simple fact that it tends to fade. Now, instead of its dominating the entire mental foreground and agitating you, you understand that it is just a temporary state. It arises because of the way your brain has been conditioned in the past. After you repeatedly realize this fact, inappropriate emotions dissolve more readily into the background, similar to the way you repeatedly observe clouds passing by and vanishing from the sky.

The Satipatthana Sutra then goes on to cite a sequence of four conventional steps in mindfulness training. Note that they involve direct experience. One is becoming mindful of the rising and falling of the abdomen during breathing. Another is noticing and making a mental note of what is actually happening, both during your formal meditation *and* during such ordinary activities off the cushion as thinking, mind-wandering, seeing, chewing, and swallowing. Another is noticing any uncomfortable sensations and continuing to notice whatever transpires during each present moment. Finally, you examine the particular emotional feeling that pervades distinct mental activities. Are you feeling doubt, regret, sadness, happiness? Chapter 11 will continue to discuss the several qualities involved in such mindful attentiveness.

Zen keeps reminding us to focus on more than the psychological problems caused by the way the Self has been conditioned. We also need to be alert to the huge problems caused by the way we use *words* [ZB: 293–298; ZBR: 229–237]. Zen itself has introduced some confusing words. Consider the Zen phrase *mu-shin*, meaning "no-mind."[3] It *doesn't* mean a vacuity, a mental blank, a state of unconsciousness. Instead, it refers to the basic clarity and receptive nature of our mind once we liberate it from discursive thoughts driven by unskillful emotional reverberations. The Korean Zen Master Chinul (1158–1210) devoted fifteen chapters to his "Straightforward Explanation of the True Mind."[4] Chinul carefully explained what this no-mind was. It was a mind *not* deluded by errant thinking. This mind could still access its full range of subtle discriminative mental functions. Thus, "no-mind" refers, not only to our being keenly aware of each present moment in a calm, clear manner, it can also include our normal allied capacities for calm, clear, objective mindful *introspection* [ZB: 125–129, 141–145].

Zen Master Dogen (1200–1253) also spoke of this kind of objective introspection. He used terms that implied one's attention was turning around, so that it could now examine one's innermost mind (*eko hensho*). Trainees cultivate this degree of calm, introspective Self-analysis in a manner so open and flexible that their general background of awareness still stays in touch with their actual living sensory experience.[5]

In the Soto Zen style of sitting meditation that Dogen brought back from China, one's thoughts are allowed to drop off naturally (*shikantaza*). One result of this repeated process of letting go is that the witness gradually develops a level of clear, intense concentration. What *is* such a level? Maezumi-Roshi describes it as being "physically relaxed and yet in a state of greatly heightened alertness."[6] Then, what does the term *no-thinking* mean at this enhanced level of concentration? Again, notice that it implies letting go of only the *emotionally biased*, Self-centered, "conditioned functioning of consciousness." No-thinking will certainly not deny all the useful functionings of one's mind.

Master Sheng-yen expressed the nature of this gradual Self-emptying process in the following way: "As the mind becomes clearer, it becomes more empty and calm, and as it becomes more empty and calm, it grows clearer."[7] At this implicit level of calm, undistractible clarity, "what decreases with stillness is not awareness of the world, but the tumult of clinging thoughts and passions that impede our awareness of it."[8]

When can our brain's innate objectivity begin to flourish? Only when our inappropriate Self-centered subjectivity begins to dissolve. Sigmund Freud was precisely on target in describing this prerequisite condition that enables our native underlying intelligence to emerge. He said that it "can function reliably only when it is removed from the influences of strong emotional impulses." [SI: 223] Long-term meditative training serves to lengthen the emotional fuse and empty the explosive charge of the negative emotions of greed and anger.

If there exists such an uncluttered, clear, stabilized mental field inside consciousness, when do meditators usually first discover it? Only when they finally begin to go on retreats (part IV). During retreats they may also become aware of one of the more dynamic manifestations associated with their *un*-conditioning. It emerges unannounced in the form of a deepened, subtly enhanced sense of mental and physical energy.

A Zen term for this development is *joriki*. The word refers to this substantial degree of clear, heightened, ongoing, stabilized mental concentration and physical competence.[9] Even though most practitioners find that this by-product of a retreat dwindles after several days, its residues persist in memory: "This is what it feels like to be *really* living!" The impression left by such a sense of resilient well-being is often far beyond that experienced after one spends the same number of days on an ordinary vacation in the outdoors.

The next chapter explores the neural basis for our attentiveness.

3

Our Two Lateral Cortical Systems of Attention

The faculty of voluntarily bringing back a wandering attention over and over again is the very root of judgment, character, and will.

William James (1842–1910), *Principles of Psychology*, Vol 1, 424

A dorsal attention network enables sensory stimuli to be selected based on internal goals or expectations, and links them to appropriate motor responses. A ventral attention network detects salient and behaviorally-relevant stimuli in the environment, especially when they are unattended.

M. Corbetta, G. Patel, and G. Shulman, 2008[1]

Why do these pages keep emphasizing attention?

Because *attention is our essential, vanguard mental function.* Indeed, attention's sharp point serves as the foremost tip of consciousness. Attention is the point that impales stimuli and anchors them. Now held fixed, they are ready to be processed as perceptions. When we use the phrase "attentive processing," it simply makes explicit the fact that *attention precedes processing.* This holds true whether we further conceptualize the forms of attentiveness as either requiring effort or being effortless, as being directed toward internal or external events, or as functioning either consciously or unconsciously (see figure 1).

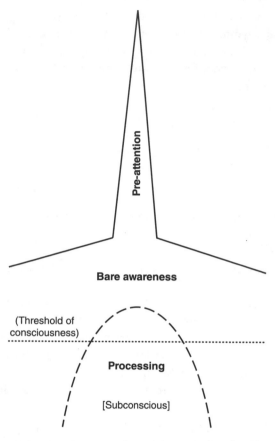

Figure 1   A visual representation of top-down attentive processing on a background of bare awareness

Attention is the sharp point out at the tip of our processing. We direct most of our attentiveness toward events in front of us, "up close and personal." We extend its sharp point toward external or internal targets. Its pre-attentive tip operates in the early milliseconds. Attentive processing follows. Only certain percepts rise to levels above the threshold of consciousness. The remainder register only subconsciously.

The fundamental role of arousal is illustrated not in figures 1 and 7, but in you the viewer, whose morning tide of tonic (sustained) arousal enabled you to wake up this day. Thereafter, novel or stressful events could prompt you into brief (phasic) arousals, and cause you to become more alert.

Attention is an associative function. Its various networks draw their resources from diverse levels in the brainstem, subcortex, and cortex. Survival values programmed their sharp preattentive tip. It now expresses an innate intelligence. Preattention has become so highly evolved that today's brains now know instantly *where* to scan for *which* kinds of top-priority information and how to relay the data through our attention channels to be processed immediately.

Research during the past decade has revealed that the higher levels of attentiveness are directed by *lateral* cortical networks. These serve two generic systems of attention [ZBR: 179–183; SI: 29–34].

Background: Attention and Awareness

As you are reading this sentence, you are probably directing your gaze *down* at a printed page or electronic screen. In this instance, the words are entering from a space *down below* your usual visual horizon when you are gazing straight ahead. Moreover, these words are entering into your peripersonal space, a relatively small envelope of space *close to your own body*.

On the other hand, suppose that you are meditating outside. There, unexpectedly, a bright planet in the predawn sky suddenly captures your attention. Now, as your head is raised, your gaze automatically turns *up* to see this bright object. It shines far out in the eastern sky, just *above* the distant horizon. It turns out that two different networks over the *outside* (lateral) surface of your cortex will have represented each of these two different systems of attention. The first system attends preferentially to external events *down* in the lower part of the space near you. You feel possessive about this space. It's your turf, so to speak. This system serves needs distinctly different from those that suddenly shift your gaze *up* to see the planet Venus.

The Brain's Dorsal Attention System

The networks of the first, dorsal, system are distributed higher up over the outside of the brain. They direct our more *voluntary*, "executive" types of focused attention, such as when you're reading these words on a page. Figure 2 shows that two major modules reside on this dorsal attention network as it arches upward to pursue a *parieto → frontal* course. The first is the intraparietal sulcus (IPS). The second is the region around the frontal eye field (FEF).

Our dorsal attention system is said to be crossed. This means that each side responds most attentively to stimuli that arrive from the spatial environment over on the *opposite* side. Moreover, these useful functions converge whenever we need to focus down on nearby things that are in front of us. We use this system's top-down functions in two ways. We use them first when we're already biased by prior cues and then make fine-tuned adjustments to the actual sensory stimuli as they next start coming in. Second, we use them to continually monitor this fresh, incoming data in order to respond to each of its new potential short-term conflicts in an appropriate manner. In general, this dorsal network helps us reach out with our hands and respond accurately during tasks that we can already anticipate are going to be reasonably well defined.

The Ventral Attention System

The ventral system was designed to serve our other attentive needs. It specializes in *reflexive, involuntary* types of diffuse attention.[2] The bottom-up functions of this ventral system respond *automatically* to each fresh need to disengage attention from whatever target it was fixed on before. The ventral system remains on standby alert. It is poised *effortlessly* to

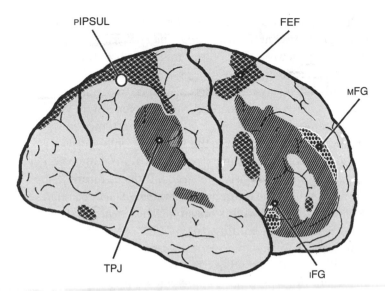

Figure 2   A lateral view of the right hemisphere showing the major modules and subdivisions of the dorsal and ventral attention systems The right frontal lobe is positioned at the viewer's right. The ventral ("bottom-up") subdivision of the attention system is shown as gray areas composed of diagonal lines. Its chief modules are the TPJ (temporo-parietal junction) and the inferior frontal gyrus (iFG).

The dorsal ("top-down") subdivision is shown in black checks. Its chief modules are the pIPSUL (posterior intraparietal sulcus) and the FEF (frontal eye field). The two pale dotted zones in the right inferior frontal gyrus (iFG) and middle frontal gyrus (mFG) represent regions of "executive overlap." They help integrate the functions of the subdivisions in practical ways that serve our global needs to attend to events on both sides of the environment.

The figure is freely adapted both from the text and from figure 5 in M. Fox, M. Corbetta, A. Snyder et al. Spontaneous neuronal activity distinguishes human dorsal and ventral attention systems. *Proceedings of the National Academy of Sciences U.S.A.* 2006; 103:10046–10051. See also the color plate facing page 168 of [SI] for a color version of this figure.

help the brain receive stimuli, detect them, and shift attention. Toward what? Toward *any kind of relevant stimulus that might enter unexpectedly*. Where might such a stimulus come from? *From either side* of the environment, crossed or uncrossed. This ventral system also has two major cortical modules. Each is represented much lower down, yet again over the *outside* of the brain. One is the temporo-parietal junction (TPJ). The other is the inferior frontal gyrus (IFG).

A key point: The functions of this ventral attention system are represented *asymmetrically*. Indeed, figure 2 shows the right side of the brain because this *right side dominates the ventral system*. How is this possible? The circuits on this right side cross over the midline to co-opt those other ventral attentive mechanisms that we represent over on the left lower side of our brain. So what? The result is that the *right lower side* of our brain assumes *a bilateral* responsibility. Its job is to respond attentively the instant any unexpected, *behaviorally relevant* stimulus—a bird call, for example—suddenly arises from *anywhere*.

These physiological properties of the ventral system serve *involuntary reorienting* functions. They are more bottom-up and reflexive in nature. *We* don't choose to direct them. *They* redirect attention instantly—as choicelessly as our leg reacts with a jerk when its knee tendon is tapped by a reflex hammer. Redirect it, to what? To whatever new stimulus happens to arrive from the vast global sensory world outside our skin. This key distinction—between voluntary and involuntary—will soon become fundamental to our discussion of the different techniques we use to meditate.

Later we expand on James's original emphasis on voluntary attention. Chapters 7, 11, 12, and 16 suggest that we engage the *involuntary* faculty of re-mindful attentiveness in the character development that evolves during later meditative training.

What's so special about the right-sided cerebral dominance of this bilateral, wide-open attentiveness?

It implies that the *right* ventral attention system is relatively free from the same heavy commitment to language with which evolution burdened similar regions of the cortex over in the opposite frontal and temporal lobes. This raises an intriguing possibility. After repeated training, could profoundly selfless insights be able to evolve wordlessly, especially if they mostly happened to be flowing through the bottom-up processing pathways on the lower right side?

How does attention differ from ordinary bare awareness?

We *direct* top-down attention toward a target. Bottom-up attention is *captured* by a fresh stimulus. Bare awareness implies a more basic, baseline level of receptivity for diverse sensate stimuli in general [SI: 14–21; ZBR: 184–187]. Event-related potential (ERP) studies help specify the ways bare awareness differs from attentiveness. For example, ERP research indicates that we first need to be deploying some kind of mental construct of space in order for our awareness to be able to detect, subjectively—at around 200 milliseconds—the *mere presence* of a faint visual stimulus that arrives within such a space.[3]

Suppose, on the other hand, that researchers define attention as tapping into our *later* processing stages—the particular functions that now enable us to go on to identify the *cognitive features* of a stimulus using our higher levels of reflective consciousness. This is a much more sophisticated event. It correlates with ERP peaks that arise 400 milliseconds after the stimulus.

Awareness of a visual stimulus causes a stronger negative afterimage than does attention per se.[4] It also tends to correlate with earlier processing sequences. These begin in the lateral geniculate nucleus and relay up to the primary visual cortex. Such an association with afterimages is of interest in relation to a negative afterimage that can occur late during kensho [ZBR: 426–428].

Are these two lateral systems the only avenues we have for attending to stimuli?

No, we also have *interoceptive* pathways that relate more subtly to our Self than do the pain pathways, which are inherently Self-centered. Other messages from our visceral organs follow an "inside passageway" that leads up through the medial thalamus to the insula. Through this route we can also attend to stimuli arising from the vestibular system of our inner ear. These messages automatically help our body remain balanced [ZBR: 95–99; SI: 253–256]. An important functional magnetic resonance imaging (fMRI) study by Farb and colleagues[5] demonstrates interesting results after only eight weeks of mindfulness-based meditative training: a decrease in the (unconscious) connections that would habitually link the right insula with the ventromedial prefrontal cortex; an increase in the connections that also link this right insula with the dorsolateral prefrontal cortex (suggesting an acquired capacity for different messages that are now more accessible to consciousness); plus a decrease in the activity of the left dorsal amygdala (which is consistent with a reduction in the meditators' emotional tone and reactivity).

4

Self/Other: Our Two Ways of Perceiving Reality

The fundamental delusion of humanity is to suppose that I am here (pointing to himself) and you are out there.
Zen Master Hakuun Yasutani (1885–1973)

Obviously, I'm here, inside my skin. Is there something wrong with my believing that you are the person out there?

No, that's the way evolution wired us. Even the one-celled amoeba needs to make a practical distinction between itself and the local environment outside it. Our brain circuits perpetuate these inherent dualities [SI: 53–64].

Our first priority goes—automatically—to our Self-centered notions of reality. This is our standard version. It frames its perception of reality with reference to our own, personal, *egocentric* processing system. We can actually feel and *see* in a mirror the face, arms, and legs of our physical Self using this personal frame of reference. We *hear* our voice in it, and *feel* our own body move. We're so familiar with this tangible, life-long frame of Self-reference that any other way of perceiving reality sounds counterintuitive. Figure 3 illustrates this Self-centered point of view.

Imagine that this person happens to be looking *down* in the act of reaching for this apple on a nearby surface. His eyes receive photons radiating from that apple and convert them into successive trains of nerve impulses. As these impulses relay quickly into the back of his brain, they do more than simply register the apple's raw visual image. They also go on to relate the 3-D position of the apple's spatial coordinates back *directly to the particular 3-D position* that corresponds with the location of the person's body image—within the schema that represents his *physical Self* in space.

Likewise, when you are the subject who looks at a real apple, your egocentric pathway also becomes part of the central physical axis receiving the apple's image because you *re*created its image with reference to your own personal three-dimensional body schema. So this Self-centered pathway doesn't simply ask *Where?* It has been beautifully designed both to (1) frame this question and (2) render a highly practical answer. It asks *"Where* is that apple *in relation to me,* back in this center of *my* world?" The common phrase, "up close and personal" assumes added significance in such a peripersonal 3-D spatial context.

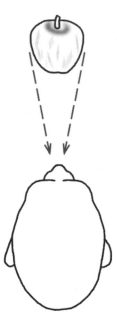

Figure 3 The Self-centered, egocentric point of view
This diagram suggests that the lines of sight point back toward the Self. They converge on the pointed nose of the subject who looks down at this apple. The nose serves as the leading edge of his own private somatic axis of Self. This 3-D construct of the person's physical Self becomes the schema that will serve as the major central frame of reference for the subject's viewing of this apple *in relation to* his own body.

Figure 4 (see color plate) illustrates why this *dorsal* egocentric pathway (**E**) proves useful when we need to hold a baby on our lap or guide a hammer down toward a nailhead. In each case, visual messages from the *upper* part of the occipital lobe speed on up through the *parietal* lobe and then leap forward into our *upper* frontal regions. These interactive networks are all action-oriented. Their metrics help us execute commands whenever we need to manipulate things held close to our body. It may help to think of this pathway as a "northern route."

However, note what else this (E) trajectory implies. It means that every top-down form of attentive processing can easily link into the nearby circuits that represent this *overlapping* construct of our own personal *physical* Self, our *soma*. Therefore, although any similar Self-centered, biased perception has assets, it also has inherent tradeoffs. They can reinforce our already heavily biased personal belief system. One thing has long been absolutely certain: *I am this independent, sovereign Self who is obviously looking (Self-consciously) at that thing down there in front of me.*

- **Your egocentric processing networks are hardwired. They are already dominant. Be careful not to overuse them.**

Why is our physical Self-image so intimately entangled with this parieto → frontal "E" trajectory?

The answer begins in brain anatomy. As Freud said, "Anatomy is destiny." Higher up in the parietal lobe, this Self-referential (E) stream enlists the services of two of our fastest, most intimate special senses: touch and proprioception. Their sensory contributions heavily bias this northern stream's priorities. Proprioception informs us subliminally exactly *where and how* all of our separate body parts coexist in space. When receptors sensitive to stretch combine with those detecting touch, the result helps us handle tangible things near our own body. Notice that whenever we use touch and proprioception to manipulate tools, utensils, or keyboards down in front of us, *we're directing our eyes to gaze down below the distant visual horizon. We are often bending our head down as well.*

There's a second, covert way to perceive reality [ZBR: 15–19].

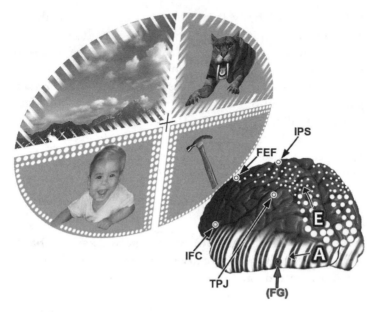

Figure 4 Egocentric and allocentric attentive processing; major difference in their efficiencies

This view contrasts our dorsal *egocentric*, top-down networks with those other networks representing our ventral *allocentric*, bottom-up pathways. Your vantage point is from a position behind the *left* hemisphere. The end of the occipital lobe is positioned at the bottom on the right side.

This brain is shown gazing up and off to the left into quadrants of scenery. (The items here are imaginary and are not all shown to the same scale.)

Starting at the top of the brain are the same two modules of the top-down attention system: the intraparietal sulcus (IPS) and the frontal eye field (FEF). They serve as the attentive vanguards for our subsequent sensory processing and goal-oriented executive behavior. Notice how they are overlapped by the upward trajectory of the *upper* parietal → frontal egocentric (**E**) system. It is shown as an arc composed of white circles. Notice that rows of similar white circles also surround the *lower* visual quadrants containing the baby (at left) and the hammer (at right). Why? To indicate that this dorsal attention system attends more efficiently to these *lower* visual quadrants when we handle

Wait. I thought there was only one true reality. Can we have two different ways to perceive reality?

Yes, we can. The pathways of this second version of reality traverse a lower compartment.[1] Its functions are so hidden that they seem counterintuitive. Still, they do provide the brain with a complementary, other-referential version. This version frames reality from an independent, *allocentric* perspective. Allocentric comes from the Greek *allo*, meaning "other" (**A** in figure 4). Its job is simply to recognize what is happening. It's organized to ask two *"what"* questions: *What is it?* and *What does it mean?* In this dual role, it first uses pattern recognition functions to identify objects, especially when they are unfamiliar. Simultaneously, parallel circuits are already starting to interpret what such items *mean*. They are even beginning to infuse nuanced *values* into the gist of *what* they interpret is "really" existing out there [ZBR: 21–22].

Suppose the objects imaged out there happen to be three apples. In this instance, the role of such an other-centered frame of reference is to represent a perspective in which

---

such important items close to our own body, aided by our senses of touch and proprioception.

In contrast, our two other modules for cortical attention reside lower down. They are the temporo-parietal junction (TPJ) and the regions of the inferior frontal cortex (IFC). (Figure 2 illustrates that this ventral region includes the inferior frontal gyrus.) During bottom-up attention, we activate these ventral modules—chiefly on the *right* side of the brain. They can engage relatively easily the networks of allocentric processing nearby (**A**). The diagonal white lines that represent these *lower* temporal → frontal networks also surround the *upper* visual quadrants. Why?

This is to suggest the ways this lower pathway is poised globally to use its specialized pattern recognition systems, based on *vision* and *audition*, to identify items off *at a distance* from our body and to infuse them with meaningful interpretations. The FG in parenthesis points to this pathway's inclusion of the left fusiform gyrus, a region hidden on the undersurface of the temporal lobe. It contributes to our complex visual associations, including the sense of colors. **See the color plate.**

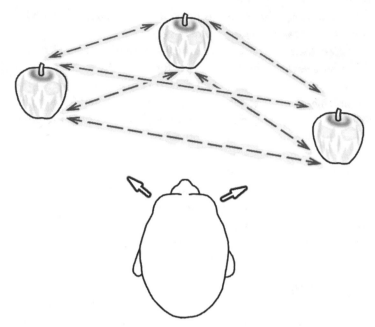

Figure 5 The other-centered, allocentric point of view
This diagram suggests that the distant apples reside "out there" in space. Here, they exist in an independent frame of reference that bears no necessary relationship with an observer. Their lines of "sight" relate to each other.

each object identified as an apple coexists in relation to the *other* apples *out there*. Notice that their lines of sight are *not* shown pointing back to the body of the subject (figure 5).

It's difficult to understand this hidden allo-compartment, hard to envision how it operates. It might help to imagine that the first apple you are seeing back in figure 3 is now in the viewfinder of *your very own* camera, a camera in which you're also acting as the lens. In contrast, imagine that those three apples in figure 5 are in a different picture on a distant wall, a snapshot taken somewhere else by an anonymous photographer who used a different camera. This is the difference between personalized awareness and awareness anonymous.

Even if one steps way back and acknowledges the notion of such an independent allocentric stream, it still proves difficult to hold on to this concept.[2] In part this is because its detached mode of attentive processing does begin so anonymously. Even so, this same anonymity retains a priceless asset: *it's highly objective*. At the start, none of our own private subjectivities intrude into this picture.

So what?

Inherent in allocentric processing per se is the impression that it is conveying a more objective version of reality. This hints at the objective role it can play when it instantly becomes the dominant mode of attentive processing during the extraordinary Zen states of kensho and satori.

This other-referential version has additional intriguing properties. Referring back to figure 4 we observe how the allocentric pathway (**A**) is pursuing its *lower* course through the brain. You might think of this as the "southern" pathway. Notice what happens when information arises from a distance. Not within our reach, but farther away from us— say, from clouds up in the sky. As this scene enters our *upper* fields of vision, it is processed *first* down in the *lower* occipital lobe. (Remember, many neural functions are crossed.) From there impulses can easily relay *down* through the temporal lobe and forward into the lower frontal regions.

The efficiencies of this lower temporo-frontal trajectory are designed to take advantage of the distance-receptor capacities of our two other special senses. These are our senses of *vision* and *audition*. They make major contributions to our other-referential associations. *What* we can see, and *what* we can hear are crucial. These senses enabled our progenitors to survive by detecting objects way *out there,* at much safer distances away from their bodies. We inherited this legacy of distant early-warning (DEW) capacities. Our DEW pathways give us milliseconds of advance notice to evaluate what things mean "out there," things much more abstract and intangible than those tangible items that we might manipulate using our fingers.

I'm more of a visual person. How important is my sense of hearing?

Your 3-D auditory skills are more globally attuned than are your visual skills. Vision perceives things in front. In contrast, hearing is keenly sensitive to even faint rustling sounds that might arise from *behind* us (say, from a sabertoothed tiger that might be lurking behind us in the remote underbrush). Multilevel refinements of such a global 360-degree awareness enable us to be more circumspect and behaviorally alert.

Let's now try to summarize the major practical points about how evolution appears to have "wired" the functions of key cortical pathways and interactive networks in the brain:

1. Pathways *lower down* in the *right* hemisphere play the dominant role in our automatic, *bottom-up* system of attentive processing. Does a precedent exist for the way this *right*-sided macro-network can be further trained to confer its global, *involuntary* mode of attention? Yes. When we learned to speak, write, and comprehend language, our representations of these dominant linguistic functions were activated more in the corresponding cortical regions of our opposite, vocal *left* hemisphere.

2. *Top-down* attentive processing operates differently. It relies on the iPS and FEF modules within the *upper,* parieto → frontal pathways in each hemisphere. These

networks help point the way for the expression of our Self-centered, action-oriented behaviors. This *voluntary* form of attentive processing is especially efficient whenever we *look down* and use our senses of touch and proprioception to manipulate tangible things held close to our own body.

3. The *lower*, occipito → temporal lobe pathways attend and process differently. They identify visual information most efficiently when its stimuli enter from more distant environments, including from scenery located above our usual visual horizon. Moreover, the temporal lobe is globally attuned to recognize and interpret patterns of sound stimuli that can arise from anywhere.

The Self/other, ego/allo distinction is fundamental. Please refer to figures 1 through 5 whenever you need to refresh your understanding of this pivotal difference between Self-centered and other-centered attentive processing. Any time we perceive the world *ego*centrically, we are embracing the sovereignty of our own subjective Self to some degree. In sharp contrast, the *allo*-centric perspective tends to remain subordinate, hidden out of sight at subconscious levels.

During meditative training—*without your being aware of it*—two developments can emerge and deepen simultaneously: (1) the *letting go,* and restructuring, of some prior habitual Self-centered attentive processing, and (2) the gradual easing toward (and rarely, a shift into) those covert, bottom-up modes of attending that emerge naturally as you revise your habits of allocentric attentive processing.

- **You won't be Self-consciously aware of, or recognize, many "signposts" along the Path toward selfless meditation. Their subtle transformations will be evolving incrementally, at subterranean levels** (chapters 19 and 20).

*Don't expect to know precisely either where you're heading, when you might happen to "arrive," or what it actually means to be "enlightened."

The "goalposts" keep moving farther on . . .

*Don't expect to approach mature levels of balanced, selfless, meditative competence until you actually commit yourself to meditating regularly and to practicing throughout the day.

Your lifelong, top-down, Self-centered habits, attitudes, and traits are too thoroughly rooted. This puts a premium on learning new ways to recognize your maladaptive Self and to let go of its dysfunctions. Thereafter, its energies can be transformed in the direction of compassion, skillfully deployed.

5

Can a Psychic Sense of Self Be Cancelled?

I know that I exist; the question is, What is this "I" that "I" know?

René Descartes (1596–1650)

The person is a conglomerate of independently functioning mental systems that in the main reflect nonverbal processing systems in the brain.

Michael S. Gazzaniga

Background: Sources of Self, Origins of Selflessness

Have various brain imaging techniques suggested where some sources of the Self of our psyche are represented?

The evidence suggests that the "Self" of our psyche emerges from a matrix of networks at widely distributed levels. Their higher interactive functions are cognitive, emotional, and subtly autobiographical in nature. You ask about the psyche. In these pages, a short answer to your question about its sources need *not* begin over the *outside* of the brain. In chapter 3, we saw that our dorsal attention network was overlapping with our somatic network (figure 2). Instead, the two largest regions referable to the functions of our psychic Self are located *deep inside* the brain (figure 6). These medial regions lie along the *inner* surfaces of its right and left hemispheres. If you point your finger to the center of your forehead, you can imagine these regions being positioned farther back inside, next to the midline. Here, one deep region occupies each side of the *medial* prefrontal cortex (mPFC). The other lies farther back along each side of the *medial* parietal region.

Several components occupy this medial posterior parietal cluster. They include the posterior cingulate cortex, the precuneus, and the retrosplenial cortex. A smaller parietal region occupies a crossroad along the egocentric (Self-centered) pathway (**E**). It lies in the angular gyrus out in the posterior part of the inferior parietal lobule.

What evidence suggests that much of our strong psychic sense of Self-identity is referable to interactions among these chiefly medial frontal and parietal regions?

1. Even under casual, passive conditions, PET scans show that these same regions already exhibit the highest resting metabolic activities in the brain. They are "hot spots." Functional MRI scans confirm their high resting activities. [SI: 53–64]. The data suggest that they could be consolidating representations of prime physiological importance. (Things you might even feel were worth sharing on YouTube, MySpace, Facebook.)

2. The medial prefrontal regions activate even further when subjects engage in tasks that are clearly inturned, introspective, and Self-relational.

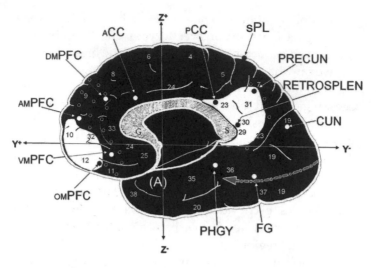

Figure 6   Two poles of a "Self-othering" axis of the psyche along the midline of the brain. Their relation to the allocentric processing stream

This view represents the inside surface of the right side of the brain. The large white area at the viewer's left occupies much of the medial prefrontal cortex. Here, normal subjects show high levels of metabolic activity in their positron-emission tomography (PET) scans even when they are resting passively. At right, the larger white area represents our second major metabolic "hot spot." It lies deep in the medial parietal region near the splenium (S) of the corpus callosum. This extensive region includes the *precuneus*, *retrosplenial cortex*, and the *posterior cingulate cortex*. The long, gray, arrowheaded dashed and dotted line represents the major initial ventral direction of the allocentric stream **(A)**. This early course of the other-referential pathway runs along the undersurface of the temporal lobe. The other A in parenthesis (A) is the amygdala. FG indicates the fusiform gyrus. The long, gray curved area in the center represents the corpus callosum. Its fibers cross over, constantly linking this right hemisphere with its partner.

3. The medial prefrontal region *and* both posterior parietal regions also coactivate during certain kinds of *inturned* Self-referential processing. This occurs especially when researchers design tasks that require such Self-inspired acts to draw on specific circumstantial environmental details that their subjects need to retrieve in order to navigate their Self through space.

These anterior-posterior coactivations suggest that some of our extended boundary concepts of Self are not exclusively referable to the medial frontal regions. Instead, their resource base appears sufficiently flexible to stretch out and include those functions one might expect during a *joint* Self/other mode of useful *co*operation. In brief, the evidence suggests that a *coalition* of components coexists. It resembles in a sense the several kinds of entries we might choose to write down in our personal journal when we are describing daily events that take place on a trip. The impression conveyed by these autobiographical operations is that our medial frontal and two parietal regions are engaging in a blended continuum of "self-othering" functions. These are the practical kinds that could integrate our psychic sense of Self into the intimate details of its immediate environmental landscape.

Back in chapter 2, the seesaw diagrams showed that external attention and Self participate in a reciprocal relationship. Does brain research actually show this inverse relationship?

Yes. Suppose you are a subject in an fMRI experiment. To begin with, even while you are partially relaxed and resting, your frontal and parietal "hot spots" are all very active. Let's say that next you are given a difficult external assignment to perform. Immediately, this catches your attention. Indeed, because you are a conscientious person, any such task will *capture* your attention. (Remember: *Where attention leads, processing can follow.*)

Now, notice what happens when the stimulus of a task turns attention "on." Simultaneously, as your networks of external attention become activated, all three of your chiefly Self-relational prior "hot spots" become "*cooler*" (become deactivated). This cause-and-effect sequence suggests that (1) the stimulus for *attention helps trigger certain other intermediary mechanisms* and (2) these in turn go on to *deactivate* a succession of the brain regions known to contribute to *your psychic Self*. In the simplest terms, attention-on, Self-off.

Similar inverse patterns can occur normally at other times. They are not limited to occasions when you respond to a task with an "attention-on" reaction. Often your resting brain's slow *spontaneous* functional MRI rhythms *also show this same kind of seesaw relationship*. However these are *very slow*, resting rhythms. They fluctuate back and forth only several times a minute. In the waking cat, direct intracranial measurements show that such spontaneous shifts are reciprocal 20% of the time.[1] In humans, during our slow reciprocal cycles of activation and deactivation, regions become "cool" that were formerly hot spots, and regions become "warm" that were formerly cool spots. Moreover, these slow spontaneous fMRI fluctuations occur in the same regions that became directly involved and activated when you were assigned a task that required you to *deliberately pay attention* or selectively engage in your Self-relational network functions.

So what?

Both the fast "attention-on/Self-off" reactions and the slow spontaneous fluctuations (in comparable regions) have profound implications for meditators.[2] A plausible initial hypothesis suggests that a deep midline structure—the thalamus—could serve as a key intermediary region. Indeed, the central location and manifold properties of the thalamus are consistent with the way it acts as a mediator between the rhythms that arise from the brainstem and those that descend from both sides of the cortex.

Three observations strengthen this interpretation. The first two support the constructs of our Self. In this sense, they represent Self-serving mechanisms. The third is of special interest to those on the meditative Path. *Its mechanisms are Self-annihilating.* They can cancel our sense of Self.

1. All nuclei in the *dorsal* tier of the thalamus normally enter into dynamic interactions with their partners up in the cortex. These stimulate the following Self-referential activities in two relevant cortical locations: (a) in the mostly medial regions just described as representing the psychic Self and (b) in those dorsal regions along the upper egocentric pathway (**E**). These represent our somatic Self (as described in chapter 4 and figure 4).

2. Three *limbic* nuclei reside at the front end of this dorsal thalamus. Their overreactivities play a crucial role in our suffering. Normally, they integrate the emotional biases received from our limbic system and then relay these valenced messages (+/–) up to influence the higher cortical levels of the Self cited earlier. All too often, what will these limbic nuclei be transmitting? Excessively charged limbic messages. These had previously *overconditioned* our Self's psychic and somatic cortical representations. The result is that such emotionally charged longings and loathings often hijack our best attempts to see the world clearly and to respond appropriately.

3. There's good news. Fortunately, the whole thalamus is enclosed in a netlike inhibitory embrace. The pivotal nucleus of the thalamus is the *reticular nucleus*. Its potent inhibitory transmitter is gamma-amino butyric acid (GABA). Instantly and selectively it can adjust thalamo ↔ cortical oscillations [ZBR: 110–112]. The reticular nucleus provides the brain with a potential seesaw capacity—a crucial way to shift its balance in both hemispheres simultaneously. In this manner, our brain can shift away from its old dominating somatic and psychic Self-centeredness and toward its other-referential modes of *selfless*, intuitive, allocentric, attentive processing.[3]

It's difficult to remember from one chapter to the next where all the lobes are, let alone how a certain remarkable inhibitory nucleus operates down in the thalamus. How about a simple explanation for a change?

Let's start with what we currently understand about how consciousness normally arises. Much in our states of consciousness depends on *which* particular blends of *oscillations* the thalamus and cortex use during their normal ongoing dialogue with each other. Normally their oscillations seem to shimmer, as it were—up and down, to and fro—at very rapid rates [SI: 87–94]. In general, when we synchronize these dynamic oscillations *in phase*, the thalamo ↔ cortical connections become stronger than when they are desynchronized and rendered out of phase with each other.

A simple analogy can illustrate how the reticular nucleus might enable a state of kensho to briefly shift *away* from our usual Self-centered frame of reference and *into* an other-referential mode of attentive processing. The contemporary active noise-cancelling headphones provide a convenient example. Only a tiny +AAA battery powers one of these headphone's electronic circuits. Even so, the circuits generate a profile of sound-wave oscillations that are 180 degrees *out of phase* with those of the undesirable background noise. The opposing peaks and valleys provide a highly selective interference pattern. It is designed to filter out unwanted sound energies such as the low rumble of traffic noise and the sounds inside an aircraft cabin. However, its tuning also enables desirable auditory signals (including music) to pass through and be heard clearly.

The thalamus and its reticular nucleus are prime candidates for diverse phenomena that arise during alternate states of consciousness. In earlier centuries, some subjects misused ether to precipitate such states. "Revelations" might emerge at a time when ether's anesthetic effects were wearing off [ZB: 237–240; ZBR: 288–296]. To Paul Blood, an American mystic, this phase of "coming to" would seem to reveal the essential "genius of being." William James also noted that such an unlimited, infinite *"existence in general"* *could awaken*—*"at a certain moment"*—*and before* one's usual Self/other dualities returned.[4]

Some sequences within such complex withdrawal phenomena dovetail with recent pharmacological research on the properties of a prototype volatile anesthetic.[5] At its peak concentration, isoflurane profoundly inhibits the reticular nucleus and the thalamic relay nuclei. Then, during the later phase of withdrawal from the gas, these nuclei recover their firing potentials. "At a certain moment," the functions of the brain's lower networks of allocentric processing could be first to recover before those that mediate Self-centered processing.

6

Gradually Letting Go of the Self

> Clean it all out! That is what this practice is for! Do a great cleaning of your mind!
>
> Shodo Harada-Roshi[1]

> When there is no self, you have absolute freedom. Because you have a silly idea of self, you have a lot of problems.
>
> Shunryu Suzuki-Roshi (1905–1971)[2]

Okay, I can see why some Buddhist teachings might propose "letting go" as a way to rid myself of unwholesome attachments and other bad habits. But letting go of my whole Self! This sounds way too radical. If I had no ego, who would stay conscious? How could I then do anything?

Meditative training preserves the basic core of your mature, adult Self-centeredness. Simultaneously, it helps you identify and cast off your many negative, maladaptive, outgrown egocentricities. This enables you to act in a more humane manner. Let's start with some ways that involve gradually letting go of the dysfunctional Self.

- **Begin each meditation period by taking a slow, deep breath in; then slowly let it all flow out.**
  This exhalation is a useful reminder: *Letting go is the essential operative mode.* Letting go is an art. It develops only after long-repeated, mindful, introspective retraining. It implies that you will be letting go of your former unfruitful, Self-centered attitudes, and will no longer be rigidly bound by them. It means that your psyche will be abandoning its former preoccupations with every Self-centered fear, fixed opinion, discursive thought, and endless need to plan ahead. Letting go means transforming your dysfunctional *I-Me-Mine* triad [ZB: 34]. This means giving up your arrogant, assertive *I*, dropping your belief that your *Me* is always a beleaguered victim, and abandoning the delusion that every possession of your *Mine* is yours in perpetuity.

- **Letting go means not striving for absolute perfection, yet still accomplishing the essentials.**
  Letting go leads increasingly toward the effortless attention and calm efficiency implied in the ancient Chinese phrase *wu-wei*.[3] Efficient behavior during everyday activities speaks volumes about how mature you have become. It implies that you have repeatedly practiced your intentionally programmed behaviors to such a degree that you are *left emotionally free of them*. Finally, you can critique them from a calm intellectual platform detached from the fray.

Gradually this ongoing detached competence evolves into a positive attitude. Its momentum helps resolve difficult tasks spontaneously. In the resulting clarity and cool objectivity, you now find yourself interacting instantly and resolving skillfully whatever new situation happens to occur [SI: 237–244].[4]

Meanwhile, what else can letting go accomplish? It serves to diminish the habitual emotional energies that would otherwise keep driving you into superficial Self-centered, mind-wandering word thoughts and other unfruitful ruminations. It also means you'll be replacing with a lighter touch those former worried hopes and fantasies about what *ought* to be.

- **Lighten up.**

Item: A recent, popular play was performed at our university. It was entitled: "I Love You. You're Perfect. Now Change." After all, enlightenment really involves "lightening up." It means you can appreciate people and things as they actually ARE, right NOW, not as "I" insist they *should* be, or must be in the future in order to suit "*Me*."

Over the decades, letting go itself becomes a fluid, ongoing, habitual expression. It unfolds almost as involuntarily as the phases of your natural independent breathing cycle and in ways that become correspondingly worthy of trust.

Can you give an example of such an involuntary form of behavior?

Suppose you have an idle moment. Perhaps in the past you would have been programmed by a habitual need to look down, reach for a cell phone, and start fiddling with its keys.[5] Instead, your gaze might now simply drift up casually to observe the clouds in the sky. And in this more relaxed state, you wouldn't be Self-consciously aware of any rationale for doing so.

- **Inhabit bowing.**
  Sino-Japanese cultures in the past were attuned to the many beneficial aspects inherent in bowing to other

persons and other places. Bowing remains an excellent way to begin one's formal practice before sitting down to meditate on a cushion. When entering the meditation hall, for example, one bows toward the altar, toward the assembly at large, and often toward one's seat as well.

- **Allow bowing to genuinely express the fact that you are letting go of your own Self.**
  Authentic bowing means that you are now — quite literally — lowering the flag of your sovereign *I*. My Zen teacher Myokyo-ni condensed in one sentence the basic attitude that permeates bowing: "Bowing means giving yourself up to what is." What *is*, exists *right now*. How did she continually embody this essence of letting go during daily life practice? She simply leaned forward briefly at the waist as she responded to each new situation [ZBR: 201–203].

- **Bow deeply from the waist as an expression of profound gratitude.**
  Consider how much you have to be grateful for! Life — right *now, just this* — is an incredible gift. Countless other ancestral beings in the biosphere contributed to our presence on this planet today. Countless others still make our existence possible. Each present moment *is* a present in itself — the gift from green plants that supply all the oxygen we breathe. Gratitude in bowing means thankfully accepting not only *what is* — warts and all — but responding gratefully for every blessing life on Earth has given us.

- **Extend your arms, wrists, fingers. Open up your gestures.**
  Simple movements of your head and trunk also constitute "body language." Experiments indicate that these other gestures, similar to bowing, favor a men-

tal shift toward a more other-oriented (allocentric) frame of reference [ZBR: 172–174]. You may become aware that similar, slight forward leanings happen involuntarily at rhythmic points of emphasis while you are engaged in chanting practices.

*Don't think that you should strive for artificially contrived movements. Rather, allow such behaviors to evolve involuntarily, unselfconsciously. They'll arrive as a natural byproduct of long-term meditative training.

- **Reorient attention, turning it outward.**
  Some beginners start to meditate with a preliminary "body scan," moving their attention successively from one part of the body to another. This preliminary technique can be useful to the degree that it helps train (an *inturned* form of) our top-down attention. Yet, many *external targets* are also available in the world outside your body. External focal points don't have the same disadvantageous tradeoffs. Choosing an external target relieves you of the obligation to pay so much effortful, focused, concentrated attention on separate regions of your whole physical body (your *soma*). Somatic preoccupations can prove counterproductive.

Recent research in learned motor skills shows that when we choose to focus attention *externally*, we function more automatically and with greater efficiency than if we attend to our own body movements.[6] Later on, when you learn to open up into more *outward*-turned, bottom-up, *receptive* modes of awareness, you'll begin to discover similar subtle assets.

We develop these topics further in the next chapter, where they become relevant to each of the two basic categories of meditation.

7

Two Complementary Categories of Meditation

> The primary sign of a well-ordered mind is one's ability to remain in one place and linger in one's own company.
>
> Seneca (c. 4 B.C.E.–65 C.E.)

> When one goes into Zen meditation, one passes as a usual process, through a psychic field, from the surface down into the depths, as if one were plummeting into a lake in a diving bell.
>
> Nanrei Kobori-Roshi (1914–1992)

As Buddhist meditation practices slowly evolved from the ancient Yogic traditions, they began to train attention in two mutually reinforcing ways. The resulting generic categories are often described now as *concentrative* meditation and *receptive* meditation.[1,2] Table 1 summarizes the two approaches.

A common way to begin seated meditation is first to *look down* and focus on a particular spot. Then one:

1. Eases into a softer, less intense degree of this down-focused visual attention.
2. Identifies the slight in-and-out movements linked to one's breathing, and follows each of them closely.
3. And continually monitors the degree to which one's attention can be maintained on one or both of these tasks.

The three examples suggest how much mental effort is required even to begin concentrative meditation practice. It all begins earlier with our *intention*. We intend to pay attention. We ourselves are the central executive agency. We set up these conscious goal-directed activities so that they can

Table 1
The Attentive Art of Meditation; Two Complementary Categories

Concentrative meditation	Receptive meditation
A more effortful, sustained attention, focused and exclusive	A more effortless, sustained attention, *un*focused and inclusive
A more deliberate, one-pointed attention. It requires *voluntary* top-down processing	A more open, universal, bare awareness. It expresses *involuntary* modes of bottom-up processing
More *Self*-referential	More *other*-referential
May evolve into absorptions	May shift into intuitive, insightful modes
Choosing to "pay attention"	A bare, choice-*less* awareness

express our top-down efforts to pay attention. We also make a mental note to monitor how consistently we can sustain our span of attention. In psychological terms, these are short-term tasks that exercise our working-memory skills. Concentrative meditation includes these several willful efforts to sharpen our focusing, select its target(s), modulate its intensity, and monitor its progress. Our choices are deliberate. We've chosen to concentrate on one small area while excluding all other items. Notice that *any level and degree* of such a voluntary approach *is inherently Self-referential.* We're always the CEO in charge.

In contrast, *receptive* modes of meditation are more nuanced. They are also much more difficult to describe, understand, and appreciate. Why? For three reasons. First, because they are entered into by a more passive, *non*-doing, open approach. Second, because they then involve minimal or zero degrees of the kinds of personal effort that can be consciously focused. Third, because their anonymous awareness taps increasingly into hidden, nonverbal subconscious resources. Later chapters (18 and 19) explain why we are largely unaware of the original depths of these resources and remind us that their elusive skills continually evolve during the more advanced stages of training.

Receptive techniques express *involuntarily*, innate varieties of bottom-up attentive processing. Why is their awareness called "choiceless"? Because no Self-conscious person is inside actively choosing what *must* be focused on, or *where* to focus. Thus, the meditator's receptivities can remain poised open. Now the brain can receive *any* stimulus that might arrive unexpectedly from *any*where. Inherently inclusive, these receptive techniques are *other*-referential, not Self-referential. Later on, figure 7 will illustrate the global extent and stimulus sensitivity of this bottom-up style of attentive processing. Compare its breadth and its array of receptors with the sharp point of the simpler top-down style shown in figure 1.

Receptive techniques open up much later into more universal kinds of bare awareness. Such a global orientation toward the "big picture" is sometimes described as a variety of meta-awareness. When such open receptivities are linked into more refined levels of preconscious processing, they tend to evolve toward more intuitive modes of understanding—into insights of various sizes. The deeper insights can plumb successive depths of existential comprehension. These tendencies have contributed to their being associated in Western Buddhism with the term *insight meditation*—a translation from the Pali word *Vipassana*.[3]

*Don't regard the concentrative and receptive categories of meditation as antithetical. However, if you allow your practice to overemphasize one category at the other's expense, such an imbalance could work at cross-purposes.

Near the start of any 20- to 40-minute period of meditation, as the visual focus first softens, one's concentration is oriented toward following each breath in and out. Thereafter, shifts occur back and forth between the two styles of meditation. They dovetail more or less spontaneously [ZBR: 214–218]. Meditation also includes episodes of mind-wandering and day-dreaming. While these are *normal* phenomena, beginners become overly concerned when they "fail" to relax and can't remain free of extraneous thoughts. They think such "simple" goals should be easily accomplished. With increasing experience, meditators realize that it is the mind's normal tendency to be discursive.

Don't be discouraged when your thoughts tend to jump around like a restless monkey in a zoo.

Learn to be much more patient with your "monkey mind." In fact, it takes a very long time for one's turbid thought stream to slow down and become clear. In the interim, you will still be cultivating a gentle, *re*-mindful art. It *returns to the appropriate focus* whenever attention seems to stray.

- **Your regular meditation practices help refine a natural reflexive capacity. After it notices a lapse, it re-mindfully disengages, and instantly returns attention to its original focus. Repetition is the key word in the art of attending with competence to its subconscious domain. Be patient; this capacity evolves very slowly.**

  Meanwhile, each lapse of attention is not a shortcoming or "failure" on your part. It simply serves to demonstrate your brain's inherent physiological resources. *They are training themselves. They are learning to notice, to shift involuntarily* and thus to *reengage themselves* in the original task. The term *neuroplasticity* is now often applied to the brain's multiple gradually Self-correcting adjustments throughout the long process of learning [SI: 37–43, 258–259].

- **Notice thought intrusions. Then observe that they dissolve.**

  Let agitated thoughts simply serve as a crude index of how much more you need to practice.

Tradeoffs occur during meditation. Each style of meditation presents its own assets and liabilities. It cannot be overemphasized that even a minimal degree of top-down processing still involves some slight volitional effort. Even when our mental and physical Self-preoccupations seem minor, they still express motivations at levels that can be Self-reinforcing. As a result, they contribute to the sum of the inherent habit energies that keep driving the internal monologue of our monkey mind. Therefore an appropriate *balance* between concentrative and receptive styles is crucial because the two are as complementary as yin and yang. Especially at the beginning will your concentrative techniques prove essential. Why? Because they strengthen and deepen your innate capacities to focus attentively with increasing intensity, clarity, and stability. Later on, some of the more refined concentrative approaches may also help you arrive at levels of increasingly vivid perception that become undistractible. These can evolve into the superficial episodes of meditative absorption [ZB: 467–518; ZBR: 313–322].

*Don't cling to the notion that an episode of blissful absorption means you are "enlightened."**

Can receptive meditative techniques develop my innate potentials to shift toward more intuitive modes of consciousness and into occasional insights?

Not in themselves. Techniques carry you only a short way on the Path.

- **Practice requires much patience, endurance, and discernment.**
  You will need plain, hard-nosed courage to diagnose your own liabilities, sheer determination to persist in any hard-slogging endeavor that requires Self-discipline, and discernment to develop wholesome new priorities.

If meditation is such a good thing, what about the observations that the later insightful states—kensho and satori—don't usually occur when one is meditating?

Yes, only very much later, and unexpectedly, do such rare moments of selfless-insight wisdom open up and become transformative (chapter 21 discusses these advanced states in greater detail). This years' long interval tends to obscure the existence of a delayed, cause-and-effect relationship between the earlier phases of a long-term meditative program and the arrival of these later states [ZBR: 7–11].

However, it bears emphasizing that no deep dissolution of Self is within your capacity to *do*. You can't think your way into it, nor can you imagine it. It *happens*. In the interim, understand that by cultivating these other-referential aspects of your regular receptive meditative practices, you will be on a time-tested Path, moving slowly in the appropriate general direction and away from your maladaptive egocentric preoccupations.

Chapters 3 and 4 raised the issue of words in relation to our left hemisphere language functions. Were you starting to suggest that our mental activities can become more selfless when they are less cluttered by words?

Yes, one can start to observe this wordless letting go of the Self after only a few weeks of regular meditation training. One may begin to notice times when—at the moment the Self-centered attachments to thoughts drops out—bare awareness per se now becomes the sole occupant of this thought-free foreground of consciousness. This first episode of stark mental clarity is an eye-opener. Even when meditators are beginning to train attention, such moments offer a glimpse of some awesome potentials inherent when a lesser Self experiences no word-thoughts. This becomes a refreshing interval of clear, enhanced awareness.[4]

Then what kinds of adjustments might gradually have been taking place, given the fact that our brain has usually burdened our Self with a heavy commitment to language functions?

This question requires a more detailed explanation.

Background: The Arrival of Self-less, Word-less Clarity

Ordinarily, word-thoughts keep bubbling up toward the surface of our consciousness. There, unused, they "pop" and vanish. Pointing out the gradual benefits of meditation, Master Sheng-yen observed that "As the mind becomes clearer, it becomes more empty and calm. And as it becomes more empty and calm, it grows clearer." Direct experience enables meditators to comprehend what this increasing clarity feels like [ZBR: 46]. Direct experience also helps meditators understand the deep meaning of other simple statements. Consider how much meaning is inherent in Shunryu Suzuki-Roshi's simple reply to one student who had complained about having mind-wandering thoughts while meditating: "When your back gets straight, your mind will become quiet."[5] When trained meditators do enter—*spontaneously*—into this same alert, heads-up-back-straight condition of thought-free awareness, it could reflect two fundamental shifts among the Self and language functions within their right and left hemispheres:

1. During Self-*less* kinds of processing, the lower temporal → frontal pathways through both hemispheres could no longer be agitated by ruminations relayed from above and driven from below. Such self-less processing could help especially relieve the *right* (attentive) hemisphere of its excessive emotionalized tendencies to cling to mental trivia and further elaborate on them.

2. During word-*less* kinds of processing, these lower temporal → frontal pathways through both hemispheres

could similarly be liberated from being constantly swept up into their usual heavy, rush-hour traffic stream of wordy, discursive thoughts. Word-less processing could also especially relieve the *left* (language) hemisphere of its habitually driven impulse to verbalize in endless semantic complexities.

What would be the short-term and long-term results of such shifts? Both lower networks (**A**) on the right and left sides could now be more free to express—in clarity—their innate, uncluttered, other-referential (allocentric) functions [SI: 64–121, 189–219]. Please refer to figures 2 and 4.

So what?
Notice that the allocentric pathway partially overlaps an important executive pathway for cognitive control. Normally this enables our frontal lobe to briefly suppress and defuse disturbing emotional memories [SI: 232–235].

How?
This pathway acts via the *right* inferior frontal gyrus (iFG). We first met this key region in chapter 3. Figure 2 shows that it is a terminus on the right lower (bottom-up) subdivision of the ventral attention system. From there, this emotional control pathway can then go on to *deactivate* incoming, disturbing sensory messages *before* their impulses can rise up through the pulvinar and the fusiform gyrus.

Very much later, suppose a long and well-trained meditator happened to drop into a major episode of spontaneous awakening. Now, during a long self-less, word-less, silent interval, its depths could have access to the resources of uncluttered networks. Finally, in an extraordinary degree of clarity, the brain could openly express its remarkable innate and insightful capacities for the kinds of involuntary, allocentric, bottom-up attentive processing that had been further refined by meditative training (chapter 21).

- Remember: It takes a long time to let go of your Self-imposed, top-down, endlessly cluttered emotional baggage.

Yes, but it's still not clear to me. How could a program of long-term meditative training enable so self-less an event to happen?

We began this discussion in chapter 5. There, we started to pass from the *outer* layers on the surface of the brain down toward the depths where major shifts take place *that can revise the axial core of the human psyche*. To answer your question, we now have to take a trip inside the neuroimaging equivalent of Kobori-Roshi's metaphoric diving bell. Our next steps descend to deeper layers within the brain. Remember that the nuclei of the thalamus will be the first crucially important stop on this descent. Down here is an array of normal mechanisms. They stand poised to switch—on and off—the ways our different thalamic nuclei interact with their partners up in the cortex.[6,7]

How can any shifts this deep transform a person's higher levels of consciousness? I thought these levels were up in the cortex.

Chapter 5 emphasized that deep shifts can revise and rechannel the oscillations within the thalamo-cortical circuits that normally subserve our states of consciousness. Simultaneously, their functions can be redirected *toward* those other-referential forms of receptivity that usually stay hidden and *away from* those standard forms of consciousness that usually imprison us in biased, Self-centered ways of perceiving the world [ZBR: 167–179].

You seem to be emphasizing two things in this long program of meditative training. One is the global scope of our basic receptivities. The other is the enhanced reactivities of our systems of attention. Why do you assign to each of these factors such an important role?

One reason is because these two openly receptive and reactive mechanisms can coincide to trigger a state of kensho. When their mechanisms converge to reshape a dynamic gateway in the thalamus, our basic Self-centeredness can drop out and our basic other-relationship can be enhanced. Chapter 2 introduced this theme of a normal inverse, seesaw relationship between external attention and egocentricity. Chapters 11, 12 and 21 will further explore some of its mechanisms.

What qualifies a Westerner who is only an M.D. to propose novel variations on meditative practices rather than the more conventional techniques that adepts in Asia have adopted for many centuries?

Most people find that meditative practices are still too time-consuming and inefficient. We need better methods. As first-year medical students, if we were not already skeptical, we quickly learned to be empiricists. Whenever we saw that a given disease had accumulated multiple treatments over the years, we realized it meant that no one treatment had provided a cure. Driven constantly to improvise more effective therapies, student physicians soon learn to value the simple therapeutic dictum: "If it works, keep doing it."

The Buddha needed no special medical degree to critique the merits of different spiritual approaches. When he visited the Kalama community, he found them perplexed by the claims and counterclaims of their prior spiritual teachers. His advice was straightforward.[8] He said to them, in effect, "No matter who says it or what you read, don't accept it without first testing it in your own experience. Test whether its effects are beneficial or harmful by the way it influences your own subsequent, everyday behavior. Does it encourage your behavior in ways that are skillful and wholesome? Or instead does it lead down the other path toward greed and hatred, causing you and others to suffer?"

- **Be ready to test different meditative techniques yourself.**

As Robert Aitken-Roshi counseled: "I am not really your teacher. You must teach yourself.... What works for you now may not work for you next year. Keep it open."[9]

Meanwhile, it's time to move beyond all these words and concepts. Let's move on toward the direct experience of meditating selflessly outdoors.

Outdoors?
Yes.

Part II

Meditating Selflessly Outdoors

I don't know anything about consciousness. I just try
to teach my students how to hear the birds sing.
Zen Master Shunryu Suzuki (1905–1971)

Returning to the Natural World

If you want to learn the nature of the world, don't study fine
bound books.
The True Jewel is in a coarse bag.
Buddha nature visits crude huts.
All those who follow the herd, clutching at mere appearances,
never seem to make the connection.

Shi Te (eighth century)[1]

Trees and stones will teach you that which you can never learn
from masters.

Saint Bernard (1091–1153)

The clearest way into the Universe is through a forest
wilderness.

John Muir (1838–1914)

*Why discuss the outdoors first as the setting in which a person
can learn to meditate selflessly? All the standard advice I've received is first to sit down on a cushion indoors.*

Brains didn't evolve indoors. When we commune with Nature,
we return to our most basic awareness—to the primal sensibility
that openly shares in just being alive. Each person's instincts are
one more expression of Nature. Nothing is more natural. Indeed, as
the last chapter indicates, when do most recorded examples of
states of awakening occur? *Not* while a person is meditating indoors. Elsewhere, later, often outdoors. And when these states do
happen, our *ego*-centric Self is transformed toward *eco*-centricity.
Every day then becomes Earth Day.[2]

Nature is our element. We open up to Nature in two different ways. We discover one way when we're outdoors.

There we become acutely aware of one of its awesome, keenly detailed manifestations—the piercing beauty of a blue columbine, the call of a bird, a spreading chestnut tree. These inspired present moments first open spontaneously when we are children. Often they happen only in solitude, when we are quiet. After Siddhartha had been worn out from his rigorous six-year quest, his memory recalled the balm of such a moment when he was still a child. *Re-mindful* of this event, he was then motivated to meditate under the Bodhi tree (chapter 11).

The second way we open up to Nature is more like the wide-open perspective seen by some ultrawide angle lens. Its capacities realize the broadest, deepest, most comprehensive insightful awareness. Deepening moments in Nature lead us to ponder the incredibly inclusive miracle we share with all other living creatures. Of course, later we often still begin to meditate with an initial misconception. Somehow we assume that we must sit indoors on a cushion. Not so. Instead, what can we discover each time we enter into a totally unaffected appreciation of our outdoor environment? There, we find that these two natural attentive processes— the first one intensely focused and concentrative, the second one openly receptive—enter into a blend of their complementary assets [ZB: 664–667].

When we repeatedly practice some task, we say it becomes "second nature." What does this imply? It suggests that we've finally let go of our top-down Self. Indeed, we've let go to such a degree that our "true nature" is finally expressed and incorporated within the original vast oneness of Nature herself.

- **Return often to the natural world. Take a walk by yourself for a change. Enjoy the solitude. Stay alert to its sounds, sights, and fragrances, to every feeling that its sensations evoke.**

Leave behind your civilized veneer. Relinquish any habitual dependence on the so-called virtual electronic scene. This message becomes increasingly important to today's generations of parents. Now they're confronted with two more perils: (1) not only the tendency to overdiagnose attention-deficit disorder (ADD), but also (2) the newly named "Nature-deficit disorder." It is prone to afflict cement-bound, urban children who have lost all contact with their biological and botanical roots.[3]

- **Raise your sights. Expand your horizons. Allow your open-eyed gaze to involuntarily drift *up* into the distance.**

  Out there, *involuntary awareness* has the potential to expand *far beyond the reach of your body*, into a whole wide world of natural scenery. Out there, *it* can observe the foliage and trunks of trees, the clouds, the whole sky. It is up there, in that apparent emptiness, that water condenses, the H_2O which makes up most of your body. Entering from up there are all those radiant solar energies that, when transformed through the energy chain, serve to power all of your activities. You and I and the rest of Nature coexist in one inseparable symbiotic kinship.

  Even so, never miss an opportunity to bend over at the waist, look down carefully, and bow to the Earth's bounty of spring wildflowers. Without looking even lower, how else could you ever discover the striking color that the wood sorrel hides on the lower surface of its leaves?

- **Sharpen every listening skill. Listen in every direction.**

  As one of Zen Master Muso Soseki's poems explains: Not from our lips do the most profound meanings arise.

Each babbling brook delivers the Buddha's sermons.
Countless thousands of poems flow, one after another, day and night,
Without a single word being spoken.[4]

- **Open up to hear to each of Nature's sounds.**
  Reflect on Shunryu Suzuki-Roshi's sage advice about how to sharpen your sense of hearing while you're on an ocean beach: "There, if you're alert, you can hear the tide turn."[5]

- **Remain alert to hear bird songs.**
  *Don't think, Self-consciously, "I'm listening to that bird."
  There's no need for you to insert your Self back into that explicit role. You don't need to be some person inside who remains actually conscious of striving to *do* the listening. Instead, allow your ears just to *hear its notes directly*. Just Hearing.

- **Consider all the other delightful surprises of becoming a bird watcher.**
  Gaze *up* to follow distant birds in flight. Notice how raptors soar effortlessly, aided by the wind. In contrast, flocks of shorebirds, like the golden plover, wheel, twist, and dive in unison. Bird sightings tap into our most primitive instincts and sentiments.[6] If you need a further stimulus to look up into the sky, take a child along and go fly a kite.

- **Let your gaze drift up to witness the ridgelines of distant hills, up toward the peaks of any faroff mountains.**
  Paul Cézanne spoke about our instinctual need to "read nature." This meant seeing *into* it, as he said, "beneath the veil of interpretation." Committed to

this endless quest, he went on to paint the lofty scenery of Mont Sainte-Victoire some *eighty-seven times*.[7]

Why do people seem inspired when they look up toward distant hills and mountains?

It does seem that the whole psyche can become inspired when we elevate our angle of vision and gaze up in the direction of distant lofty peaks or toward the sky in general. William Blake (1757–1827) seemed aware of a similar tendency. Inscribed in his *Notebook Poems* was this sentence: "Great things are done when men and mountains meet; this is not done by jostling in the street." The whole phenomenon invites thorough neuroscientific study.

- **Go out on a clear night, in solitude. Gaze up.**
  Become aware of the moon, of the immense night sky, of its planets, stars, and constellations. To Zen Master Dogen (1200–1253), "the best mental exercise for letting go of one's egotism" was to contemplate one's impermanence. Considering the billions of years the current universe has existed, the billions of humans now on Earth (and the countless species that have perished), is one transient Self on this small planet really so all-important?[8]

- **If you happen to awaken before dawn, go outdoors.**
  Gaze *up*. In a clear eastern sky, when no buildings stand in the way, you'll often find the planet Venus at her brightest. Each December 8, Buddhists worldwide still celebrate the legend of what happened when a man called Siddhartha once *looked up*, saw this same "morning star," then suddenly became enlightened. Could something dawn on you — that the stimulus at the onset of this legendary moment of "awakening" might have a remote bearing on the way you practice meditation?

When people are outdoors and look up, don't other qualities also seem to enter into conscious experience?

For centuries, it has been recognized that sublime influences are implicit in natural settings. Monks in old China and Japan held outdoor moon-gazing retreats. Poets, too, extolled the virtues of gazing up at the moon, often at those times when a harvest moon—low on the horizon—appeared to attain its fullest diameter and clarity.[9]

Trees continue to be important. The Satipatthana Sutra recommended three secluded settings as sites for one's solitary meditation: a forest, the base of a tree, and an empty hut.[10] Research reveals that normal people grow calmer when they gaze *up* toward trees that have spreading canopies. This effect seems especially impressive in the springtime when trees leaf out in bright green colors.[11] Recently, Berman and colleagues found that the students who went out for a leisurely walk through a secluded, tree-lined park (the Ann Arbor Arboretum) improved their performance scores over those on an earlier cognitive task.[12] In contrast, those students who had walked the same distance through heavy city traffic reduced their scores, suggesting that their urban experience had depleted their top-down attention functions.

- **A big old tree is one of Nature's gifts. Yield to any impulse to reach out and hug a tree. It's good practice for reaching out of your insular state and sharing hugs with other significant persons.**
  Planting a tree will add a little more oxygen for others to breathe.

Part III will say more about why looking *up* is different from looking down.

Part III

Meditating Selflessly Indoors

In zazen, leave your front door and your back door open. Let thoughts come and go. Just don't serve them tea.

Zen Master Shunryu Suzuki (1905–1971)

Settling Down and In

> Zen is not about being irresponsible and ignoring things; it is about being able to remain unattached, about seeing clearly, and beginning again, and letting go of the mind that hungers on something over and over again.
>
> Shodo Harada-Roshi[1]

> Look directly. What is this? Look in this manner and you won't be fooled.
>
> Master Bassui Zenji (1327–1387)

These were Master Bassui's dying words. The word *what* was in his final message. Fortunately, we're alive and still able to breathe in and out. During all those years in our past, our brain kept filing away details—the who-what-when-and-where circumstances of things that were happening to us. Events that entered this daily "journal" were heavily biased as soon as they passed through the Self-centered filter of our own frame of reference. These Self-tagged entries form memory traces often called engrams. Personal engrams are not trivial facts in the abstract. They don't record just any old scenic details. Collectively, they establish a private psyche, a hungry-minded Self. Our *I-Me-Mine* operations become personalized. They convince us that such a personality must possess its own separate existence. They cause us to grasp hard at life while still fearing death, and even to hope for some kind of an afterlife.

Our private memory bank contains clusters of detailed associative links fused with feeling tones. They help us remember: "*I* graduated from *this* high school, and with *these* guys and girls, this many years ago. *This* church is where we were married. We went to *this* place on our honeymoon.

This is how I *re*construct *my* whole life narrative and condense it to explain who *I* am to a stranger." And any time this Self needs to navigate within its current or old neighborhoods, it's relatively easy to access and retrieve detailed memories of the surrounding scenery.

Every personal Self carries huge burdens of this stuff. Such a "Self" is an elaborate psychic construct. Its scaffolding is an associative clutter of intangibles erected around a tangible physical axis. How can any three-pound brain possibly index, distribute, and store all this excess historical baggage yet still access precisely *what* we need at *just this* instant? It's no simple matter to maintain all these personal journal entries, yet still allow only a select few to be retrieved. Only vast, highly sophisticated networks can integrate such a Self-other continuum. Consider how much energy these networks need. Even at rest, our small brain (only 2% of our body's weight) consumes disproportionate resources of metabolic energy (some 20% of the total) in simply maintaining all of these ongoing baseline functions.

In contrast, suppose you were to volunteer to be a subject for a neuroimaging study. You learn that you'll be assigned an urgent, highly complex cognitive task. In order to solve it quickly, you'll first need to screen through a huge number of your prior associations, then select and work with only a few. This will be a difficult voluntary attentive processing task. How much more than your *baseline* energy requirements will you now need to mobilize? Only a small fraction: usually less than 3% [ZBR: 193–200; SI: 70–76] (chapter 5). As Marc Raichle emphasizes,[2] this evidence points to the vast intrinsic resources that our brain already devotes to its ongoing *involuntary* modes of processing.

Unfortunately, you have also squirreled away lots of the other irrelevant historical stuff that has cluttered up your association networks. This is in addition to your worries about dire threats that never materialized, plus the contaminating fantasies that keep projecting themselves into an imaginary multitasking future. Later on, when you sit down and try to meditate, these attached emotions will generate some of the distractions that agitate your monkey mind and prompt it to leap from one branching thought to the next. Such discursive scenarios are one reason why the ancient Zen adage advises: "Forget about the branches—get to the underlying root."

Meditation helps you unearth these underlying, subterranean issues. When you meditate, you have time both to *experience* these issues and to identify their fictitious nature. Meditation introduces a refreshing pause: control/alt/delete. The pause serves to interrupt your hectic, multitasking approach to life [ZB: 367–370]. It substitutes a more passive activity, a *relaxed attentive* state. Now, in relative quiet and solitude, three procedural sequences have time to develop. The longer you practice, the more spontaneously they unfold.

- **At first, you settle "down and in."**
  You begin as usual, by gazing *down* to focus on some discrete spot in front of you, say at an angle of around 45 degrees. Your legs assume their usual posture, adopting positions that you can maintain without unusual discomfort. Each of us begins with different physical requirements.[3] You take care to attend to the erect posture of your head and trunk. What is the "correct" erect posture? For Kobori-Roshi's trainees, it would mean "backbone straight, chin down, head back"—as though a long steel rod were extending "straight down your spine into the center of the earth and then straight up again high into the sky."

Next, you take one deep breath—slowly in and slowly out. Take more if necessary, because you're now not only letting go but also taking special care to identify *which* rising and falling movements—far down in your lower abdomen—are the ones that accompany each in-and-out breath. You register these subtle movements, then anchor their discrete low site of origin clearly in memory. These faint movements compound your senses of touch and proprioception. Later, they will remain the blunt focus of awareness after your initial focused attention softens.[4,5]

When you say "down and in," are you referring to this usual tendency to actually begin meditation by deliberately focusing my attention down and in, on this particular lower midline part of my own body?
Yes.

Why this focus down on the lower abdomen? It's easier to feel the airflow begin higher up through my nasal passages. I'm also aware that my chest expands and contracts during breathing.
True. However, when you register the in-and-out movements down in the lower abdomen, this displaces attention to a site far *away* from your head and chest. Head and chest are already the major sensory reservoirs for our notions of physical identity. They are also regions charged with emotional tension that reflect our subconscious feelings of anxiety [ZBR: 477, notes 3 and 4]. You're under no rigid obligation to *pay* attention solely to any one airflow site while you are meditating. Discover which methods work best for you. (You will still be left with ample opportunities to experience which sensations localizing in parts of your body are the signals linked with your particular emotions.)

- **Then allow yourself to experiment with different ways to follow your breath.**
  A standard *preliminary* step in training your top-down form of attention is to label each part of the breathing cycle in a way that distinguishes the phase

of breathing *in* from the phase of breathing *out*. A simple "just this" approach represents a variation of the usual silent, one-to-ten counting system [ZBR: 33–37; SI: 11–13].

For example, let its sequences begin by first prolonging the silent word "JUST . . ." throughout each *in*-breath. J-U-S-T signifies that your attention is now focusing on "Just" (on *only*) a single silent *number*—from one to ten—during each of your next ten expirations.

Similarly, prolong each of these numbers throughout the entire out-breath. This enables each breathing cycle to resemble:

J-U-S-T W-O-O-N-N; J-U-S-T T-O-O-O; J-U-S-T T-H-R-E-E, etc.

After the next sets of these numbers (1 to 10) fade, change the first word. Now prolong the word "THIS . . ." throughout each in-breath, following it with the same series of ten numbers on the out-breath. T-H-I-S-S also takes on a specific meaning. It signifies that your attention will now be focusing on only *this* next particular number.

Because you have stretched out *both the words and the numbers*, each successive breathing cycle now fully occupies your entire mental field. No mental space remains at either edge into which any extraneous, discursive thoughts can intrude.

As your random thought energies slowly recede, the ordinary rising and falling movements down in your lower abdomen can increasingly occupy the perceptual foreground of your attention and awareness. The above sets of word-numbers will also fade. At this point, introduce two more changes. First, let "J-U-S-T" return to be the silent beginning word that fully occupies each in-breath. Second, let "T-H-I-S" move over to replace each of the numbers. "T-H-I-S" becomes the new label for each out-breath, and closes each breathing cycle.

You may find it useful to reserve a particular meaning for JUST THIS. Let it signify that *only this* particular moment exists, right NOW, within a vast expanding awareness. This mental field is now free to open into the whole wide world. Its psychic contents have been reduced toward *just this* exquisite simplicity. Likewise, awareness of almost all of your physical Self has also been fading because it has been reduced to just each faint rising and falling movement down at the distant site of your lower abdomen.

After a few rounds of J-U-S-T T-H-I-S, both words also tend to fade out by themselves into your general awareness of each present moment.[6] Now your mental field can become relatively clear and thought-free to register just those faint movements down in your lower abdomen. There, let each in-and-out signify the universal life force as it happens to express itself in this one body's innate rhythm of breathing. You simply allow this faint natural rhythm to blend into the open mental foreground. All of your temporary discursive stuff has dropped out of this field of awareness.

Ultimately, during deep meditation, even the sense of a breathing rhythm in your lower abdomen can drop off. At this point, "all" that remains is Awareness per se.

- **On some other occasion, as you settle down and in, begin to experiment by opening up the posture of your hands and arms.**
  Discover — while off by yourself — the increasing degrees of freedom that can arise when you adopt a posture more open than usual. The term *openness* conveys a sense of liberation. Openness applies to both your physical posture and to the open attitude that pervades your mental posture.

For example, when we sit on a cushion, our thighs are usually rotated externally to some degree. Ideally, this could leave ample space for our lap and upper chest to become open and unencumbered. What happens instead? We adhere to the customary instruction: "Bring both hands together on your lap, overlap your fingers, and touch both thumbs." As a result, our shoulders now turn in, and the flexion posture of our arms, hands, and fingers compromises this potential space.

Try a more open posture. It is less artificial.[7] Begin by *un*flexing your wrist and fingers. Next, allow both hands to drift free from any cramped position on your lap. (Let go of the idea that such a position might have seemed to embody some "cosmic mudra," ellipse, or other related concept.) Now, *externally* rotate both forearms. This allows them to approach a posture of supination. As your elbows extend, the back of each open hand and unflexed wrist now rest comfortably farther out on top of your thighs. They no longer invade the center of your lap.

At this point, both shoulders are also free to rotate externally and to move farther back. Neither shoulder turns in to cover the front of your upper chest. These four adjustments allow you to assume a more receptive physical posture. It is natural, open-handed, and erect. It also inclines you toward an alert, heads-up mental attitude. Your sitting is poised on a threshold, ready to openly receive and accept whatever stimulus might enter unexpectedly from either side of the environment.

This is an optimal body-mind posture. It is poised to react efficiently to any fresh stimulus, consistent with the *global* functional domain of the *right* temporo-parietal junction (TPJ)[8] [SI: 262] (figures 2 and 4).

Background I: The Influence of Arm Postures

Proprioceptive signals from parts of the body act as cues. They influence our emotional feelings (+/−), our sense of familiarity, and our experience of how much effort is involved. When one's arms are in a posture of flexion, does this create a subtly different subjective effect than when they are in a posture of extension? The result depends on the general social and cultural context. Thus, in Western interpersonal contexts, arm-crossing is interpretable as a kind of defensiveness and a distancing from the other person. A recent study of forty-one undergraduates examined the influence of arm position in a different context—that created during an achievement test.[9] In this instance the subjects were under pressure to achieve a desired result. The students who deliberately crossed their arms persisted significantly longer (more than 20 seconds longer) in fruitless efforts to solve an *unsolvable* anagram, in contrast to the students who extended their arms over their thighs. The authors note that this kind of stubborn persistence is counterproductive because it wastes time and effort.

The students' next task was to find as many separate words as possible inside anagrams that could be solved because they were only *moderately* difficult. The arms-crossed students again persisted more than 20 seconds longer in the course of which they discovered a few more words than did their cohorts.

Students who persist in this achievement context are making a sustained effort to focus top-down attention on a well-defined task. It reflects their Self-centered and positive desire to succeed, and/or a similarly Self-centered (negative) unwillingness to fail. The flexed arm (and flexed hand postures) that one might assume during top-down efforts to concentrate may be less appropriate when one enters into a bottom-up, openly receptive meditative context. Try out the different postures. See what works for you.

Well, having now discussed ways I can follow my breath and allow my arms to open out, what's going to happen to my initial visual focus?

It's going to further soften and blur, but that's O.K. Meanwhile, your awareness still continues to follow your breath, and keeps returning to this anchor after each episode of mind-wandering. Finally, at long last, you'll settle down, both mentally and physically.

Then you will discover—through *direct experience*—what this state of passive, clear alertness *feels* like. In clarity, you'll learn that (1) you can be aware of your breathing cycle without recourse to the temporary crutch of concepts, numbers, or words and (2) you can also begin to feel sufficiently relaxed and mentally composed to proceed to the next stage.

This next stage will proceed to open up the brain's receptivities. To what? To intercept any visual, auditory, or other sensory stimulus arising from anywhere. We'll introduce the topic here, then discuss its receptivities further in the next chapter.

> • **During this next stage, you'll be experimenting with "turning up and out" almost everything about awareness that you had previously been turning down and in.**

So now, as a preamble to this next example of the "letting go" approach, simply allow your eyes to drift gently upward. Simultaneously, allow attentiveness to accompany your gaze. It too drifts slowly upward and outward, as it were, off into the distance.

What does "outward" attentiveness mean? Does outward define one aspect of a receptive form of meditation? Does it also suggest becoming oriented toward stimuli that could arise farther away from my physical Self back here in the center?

Yes, to both questions. However, note that we've only just begun to discuss the combined sensorimotor aspects of visual openness. Here the phrase "turning up and out" serves as a hint. It implies that several kinds of bottom-up attention can be entering into allocentric processing during a receptive form of meditation.

Background II: Why Is "What?" Important?

By way of a further introduction to the next chapter, let's briefly review the discussion in chapter 4. It explained what this other-referential processing can accomplish as it proceeds on a "southern" route along the lower temporo → frontal pathways (figure 4). Recall the normal role of these pathways. It was to ask the basic question: *What*? And recall too that at the start of this chapter, Master Bassui was also asking the same direct question: *What is this*? He took care to remind us in his final words on earth that *What*? is a crucial question.

Why has Zen discourse flourished with such one-word penetrating questions [SI: 47]? Perhaps because each question exposes the two sides of a basic paradox: true, we're on an ongoing quest for direct, clear, objective comprehension. Yet we're still stuck in the same old rut: the fundamental, "don't-know" state of ignorance inherent in any exclusive Self-centered frame of reference.

Zen masters have not only been asking the *What* question of their trainees for centuries, they have also been recommending that their trainees ask themselves *What*? during their daily life experiences. *What*? points its questioning finger toward a particular kind of answer. An important point: This answer highlights the specialized role of our *lower* pattern-recognition systems. Their distinctive resources reside within the temporal lobe. Network systems here stand poised instantly to help resolve the *What* question [ZBR: 152–157; SI: 146–152].

What is the primary job description of these temporal lobe networks?[10] The answer is immediate: *Their job is to identify stimuli—by sight and sound—wherever the stimuli come from.* In the earliest milliseconds of this specialized role, these other-referential (**A**) pathways require no sovereign Self intruding into their synapses, no private person who insists on being personally informed. Nor, while first engaged on such an independent mission, must their pathways articulate a formal word label that attaches to every coded meaning that has just been recognized.[11] Indeed, the flavor of such ineffability becomes one of the singular defining aspects of the state of kensho [ZB: 24, 547–548]. From this overview platform arises the later comprehension that "the path of words has been cut" [ZBR: 360].

The next chapter continues to explore the intriguing physiological implications of looking up and out . . . wordlessly. . . .

10

Looking Up and Out

> I will lift up mine eyes unto the hills, from whence cometh my help.
>
> Psalm 121 (King James Version)

> Keep your mind clear like space, but let it function like the tip of a needle.
>
> Master Seung Sahn (1927–2004)

How do many spiritual seekers become inspired? Often by lifting *up* their eyes—toward the hills, and also into the clear space beyond. Rarely is this "eyes up" gaze posture commented on. Yes, of course, one's erect posture is rightly emphasized. So is letting go, and following the breath. But how often do meditators receive specific suggestions about how they might elevate their gaze? And of what they might see? Curious omissions, considering their potential importance. . . .

- **Allow yourself to experiment with where and how you allow your gaze to rest.**
  Cultivate practices that enable you to look up and out. Choose a time when you're fully awake and alert. Again, begin by following the usual convention: looking down at an angle of around 45 degrees, fo-

cusing your open-eyed, top-down attention on one spot. Continue with 5 to 15 minutes or so of this usual settling down and in. All during this time you're re-mindfully aware of the rising and falling movements linked with abdominal breathing.

Now, let several things happen:

1. First, allow your *upper lids* to drift three-quarters of the way down. Yes, these overhanging upper lids will block most of the light from entering your pupils. At this point, almost all of your patterned external vision disappears. The vision remaining in the gap between your eyelashes begins to soften and blur.

2. Then, as before, allow your *gaze* to drift upward, *slowly and gently.* Initially, it might help to imagine that both eyes are *looking up and out* through your lids and far beyond your eyebrows as if to see the clouds way out in the distant sky beyond.

But, let's say you are now *indoors* and gazing up from inside your mostly closed lids. So, you're simply looking up and out into a mostly dark, vacant, visual field. This is a lids-down, elevated gaze posture. It has several potential advantages:

a. It provides an interval of rest[1] for the *lower* visual pathways. Figure 4 shows the normal role of these lower pathways. *What* kinds of things do their pattern recognition functions identify most efficiently? Things processed visually in our *upper* visual fields. This is how we recognize the outlines of hills and the actual shapes of clouds high in the distance.

b. Starting with this position of gaze now elevated above the horizontal, it's easy to *raise your chin up* slightly. Notice that you now find your *head tilting back* to follow this inclination. Simply allow this chin-up posture to evolve further into a "heads *up*," elevated posture of open receptivity. The retraction of your head has several practical consequences. First, your head becomes more erect as your neck extends straight and "tall." This encourages you to lean back at the waist and to allow the rest of your spine also to assume a more erect posture. The result is a more alert, expectant attitude in general.

   c. Some light energies can still flow in from the world outside. This light filters *through the gap between your lids* and keeps stimulating your *thin lowest edge of vision*. Zen traditions emphasize at least some degree of open-eyed meditation as a way to reduce the tendency toward drowsiness [ZB: 582].

I've always been advised to look down. The point was to keep my attention focused on some small spot that lies relatively close to my own body. Why introduce "far out" concepts that involve gazing up and looking out into space at a distance?

Looking down is a good way to *begin*. However, remember that one's meditative practices keep evolving. It is in the nature of Zen to explore seemingly novel and unorthodox techniques [ZB: 110–125, 668]. Moreover, Zen historical annals document many "triggering" episodes. These are the occasions when an unanticipated stimulus has catalyzed a major reaction from the brain [SI: 109–121]. As this stimulus captures attention, the further spread of signals enhances the brain's latent potentials to shift into a major "peak experience" [ZBR: 303–306].

In Zen, although these extraordinary states of *kensho* or *satori* are rare, they are not as novel as they might first appear. Indeed, many could be briefly expressing the higher amplitudes and coherence of a meditator's normal tendencies to shift toward other-referential sequences. These innate sequences had previously been hidden, their normal functions held subordinate to that person's top-heavy layers of dominant Self-referential processing [ZB: 491, 533].

How could a relatively simple visual or auditory triggering event shift a person's attentive processing into such major allocentric states of selfless insight-wisdom?

Several sensorimotor mechanisms normally converge each time we look *up*. Their contributions could combine to help precipitate some states of selfless awakening[2] [SI: 113–116]. In this regard, it becomes of interest to recall the old legend. What event precipitated the Buddha's awakening? It was said to have been triggered before dawn. At that particular moment he happened to look *up* and saw the bright morning star (the planet Venus).[3]

- **Remember: top-down attention is most efficient in focusing on targets down in front of you. This "conelike" convergence of visual attention (figure 1) is very different from the vast visual and hearing space that can open up to receive stimuli that arise from events far out there in the distance** (see figure 7, page 83).

Let us explore what is involved when we look up and out into distant space, yet keep reminding ourselves to balance this suggestion with other needle-sharp words of advice. Indeed, Master Seung Sahn's epigraph at the start of this chapter emphasizes our need to train *both* our pointed and our more global functions of spatial attention processing. The long-term result? An ongoing attitude of global alertness that discerns relevant subliminal clues.

Background I: Looking Up and Out

If an incoming stimulus from what we see could help trigger these rare states, then do our upper and lower visual fields normally fulfill different sensory roles?

Yes. Review the color plate of figure 4 and its caption.

And is the motor act that enables us to gaze up and off into the distance different from the act that enables us to converge the eyes while gazing down at something close to our body?
It is.

Innate physiological skills enable us to "see" *what* we "see" in visual space. We acquire other visual skills through conventional techniques that we absorb by imprinting from our culture.[4] Thereafter, we learn to discriminate and refine our other pattern recognition skills through repeated random experiences as well as through deliberate forms of training.

At the University of Florida in Gainesville, researchers on Kenneth Heilman's team have shown that our right and left cerebral hemispheres exhibit different attentional biases. These normal physiological biases combine their operations at both the *sensory-receptive* and *motor-activity* levels.[5] Certain visual performance skills of our *right* hemisphere turn out to be biased in ways that become highly relevant to the allocentric theme throughout our present discussion.

Be more specific. What are the conditions during which my right hemisphere's normal sensorimotor mechanisms are so biased that they can attend, and perform, with greater efficiency?

1. When the visual target is located up to the *left* and stimulates your *left upper visual field*

2. When this *left* upper visual target is located off at distances increasingly *farther away* from your own reaching hand.

Do any other normal physiological biases also involve my upper fields of vision?
Some do. For example, other research indicates that when we look at an object with both eyes open, we show a curious, innate

visual bias. It leads us to normally assume that this object is already being subtly illuminated by a "prior" *external* source of diffuse light.[6]

You're kidding. I've never noticed this. From which direction does this innate, "prior," source of diffuse illumination seem to come?

It too appears to originate (a priori) from up in the *left upper quadrant of our vision.*

Not until early in 2009 did I stumble across this interesting phenomenon. Since then, I've begun to take more careful notice of what my upper and lower fields of vision still "*see*"—under eyelids closed some three-quarters or so— during my regular early morning meditation. This practice begins by allowing the gaze position of the eyes to become elevated *slowly and gently.* Both eyes simply drift upward some 30 degrees or so above the line of the visual horizon when my head is erect. At this time, they are gazing up into that same dark field, under partially closed upper eyelids, that has just been described.

That's not all. Looking *up* also encourages my chin to rise and helps move my head farther back into a more erect position on my neck. The net impression during such a position of *upward* gaze is that its momentum also tends to lead the posture of my head-neck-and-spine toward a more spontaneous attitude of *open receptivity.*

Then within the first minute or so of largely receptive meditation, a diffuse play of colors often begins in the darkened fields of vision. The colors begin at the blue-green end of the spectrum and then evolve in cycles through reddish-pink toward purplish blue, violet, and purple hues. A soft wave of mental relaxation and physical ease often accompanies the first onset of the delayed violet phase.

What do color phenomena have to do with a physiological bias?

Whereas the colors sometimes begin more centrally, they usually go on to become more saturated, chiefly in the *left* upper quadrant of the darkened visual fields. Here they coincide with a subtle background luminosity.

What could cause such color saturations and luminosities to favor a person's left upper visual field?

They could be attributable to the normally greater activity within visual networks located lower down in the back of the opposite, *right* hemisphere. In this instance, the left-lateralized visual phenomena might seem to express a kind of background hum, as it were. For example, this could be a by-product of some normally greater activity arising among the opposite pathways of the *right* ventral allocentric stream as it flows on through the lower regions (**A**) of the *right* occipital and temporal lobes (please refer to figure 4).[7] On this right side, the fusiform gyrus (FG) is included among the regions sensitive to colors.[8]

Do any other visual phenomena referable to the right side of the brain also tend to lateralize more to the left side of the visual fields?

Paintings by Western artists have been cited as evidence of a similar tendency. In the past, many painters also represented their *source* of light as having originated from a region on the *left* side of their paintings.[9] In the study cited, the analysis was based on 659 paintings from the Louvre in Paris. The works were painted during the period from the thirteenth to the nineteenth century. The paintings representing these centuries were first sorted into two categories: portraits (194) and nonportraits (465). Most of these nonportraits were outdoor landscape scenes.

Huge differences emerged. The artists in these earlier centuries were 8.6 *times* more likely to have painted the illumination in their portraits as arising from a source off on their *left* side rather than from a source off on their right side. Their other (mostly landscape) paintings were also more likely (some 2.9 *times* more likely)

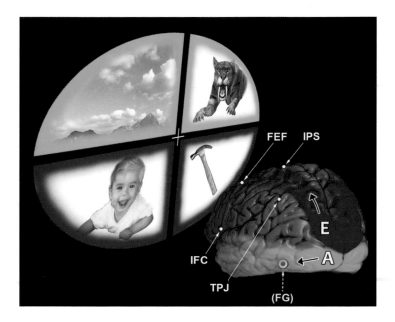

Figure 4 Egocentric and allocentric attentive processing; major difference in their efficiencies

This view contrasts our dorsal *egocentric,* top-down networks with those other networks representing our ventral *allocentric,* bottom-up pathways. Your vantage point is from a position behind the *left* hemisphere. The end of the occipital lobe is positioned at the bottom on the right side.

This brain is shown gazing up and off to the left into quadrants of scenery. (The items here are imaginary and are not all shown to the same scale.)

Starting at the top of the brain are the same two modules of the top-down attention system: the intraparietal sulcus (IPS) and the frontal eye field (FEF). They serve as the attentive vanguards for our subsequent sensory processing and goal-oriented executive behavior. Notice how they are overlapped by the upward trajectory of the *upper* parietal → frontal egocentric (**E**) system. It is shown as an arching red pathway that begins in the upper occipital region. Notice that a similar red color also surrounds the lower visual quadrants containing the baby (at left) and the hammer (at right). Why? To indicate that this dorsal attention system attends more efficiently to these *lower* visual quadrants when we need to handle such important tangible items down close to our own body. Contributing to our close-in skills are our parietal lobe senses of *touch* and *proprioception.*

In contrast, our two other modules for cortical attention reside lower down. They are the temporo-parietal junction (TPJ) and the regions of the inferior frontal cortex (IFC). (Figure 2 illustrates that this ventral region includes the inferior frontal gyrus.) During bottom-up attention, we activate these ventral modules — chiefly on the *right* side of the brain. They can engage relatively easily the nearby networks of allocentric processing (**A**). The green color used to represent these *lower* temporal → frontal networks is also seen to surround the *upper* visual quadrants. Why?

This is to suggest the ways this lower pathway is poised to stay globally alert to detect stimuli at a distance farther from our body. Moreover, when it does so, it will use its specialized pattern recognition systems of *vision* and *audition* to identify these items and to infuse them with meaningful interpretations. The yellow FG in parenthesis points to this lower pathway's inclusion of the left fusiform gyrus. This region, hidden on the undersurface of the temporal lobe, contributes to complex visual associations, including our sense of colors.

to appear illuminated from their *left* side rather than from their right side.

However, having peaked between the sixteenth and the nineteenth centuries, this left-sided bias for lighting then changed. After that, the European artistic preference for a left-sided source of illumination slacked off. The evidence suggests that painters began to question their earlier cultural assumptions, felt free to drop some very long-held, fixed artistic conventions, and began to express their individual preferences. Could some other cultural conventions, held earlier with regard to meditative techniques, also be sufficiently flexible to evolve over time? Could they too develop along lines more consistent with underlying physiological principles and individual differences?

Photographers also express preferences for their source of illumination. This is especially true when they arrange the lights indoors and deliberately pose their subjects for portraits. Did similar biases exist among photographers late in the twentieth century? I encountered individual preferences, not a consistent left bias, in a random, brief, nonrepresentative survey of world-class photographers.[10]

Background II: References in Zen to Open-Eyes, "Open-Ears" Meditative Practices

Master Shodo Harada is the highly regarded abbot of Shogen-ji in Okayama, Japan. In two cogent sentences he sums up why vision and hearing are so crucial to Zen meditation: "The senses, particularly sight and hearing, provide the most basic link between the outside world and the activities of the mind. Unless we learn to integrate each such sensory input with our zazen, our training will be of little practical use."[11] Sight and hearing are most refined in our temporal lobe networks [SI: 143–152].

Master Nanrei Kobori (1918–1992) introduced me to Zen training in Kyoto. He began his instruction by hinting at the immense volume of coexisting space that envelops me: "Breathe all the universe in; let it all slide back out" [ZB: 65]. Later, as described by Milton Moon,[12] Kobori-Roshi began a week-long training period with specific instructions. Please notice *where* he is advising the trainees to look. It is *not down* at a spot nearby. It is farther away: "At first, I do not want you to focus on things close to you, but on something preferably a little distance away—perhaps on the other side of the room in which you sit."

Finally, on the last day, Kobori-Roshi emphasized the trainees' sense of hearing. Notice how this later phase of their auditory instruction addressed two crucial points. The first point illustrates the fact that auditory stimuli might enter from *anywhere* out there in the environment outside their body. The second is with reference to the fundamental distinction between ego- and alloprocessing—to that interface which separates our Self-centered awareness from an other-centered awareness.

He began by inviting his trainees to imagine a sound. From where could such a potential sound enter? From anywhere in the 360-degree world all around us (see figure 7). Therefore this imagined sound could "be behind your forehead, or the back of your head, or close to your left temple, or left ear, or your right temple, or right ear. . . . What we are doing is nothing more than learning to train both our other-awareness and our self-awareness." [sic] *Both.*

Master Sheng-Yen (1930–2009) advocated the approach of "silent illumination" on the long path toward becoming goal-less. This practice (Chinese: *mozhao*) begins in a setting that encourages mental silence, and it emphasizes the art of first letting go of one's preoccupations. It is important to stress that this sustained silent approach will later enable

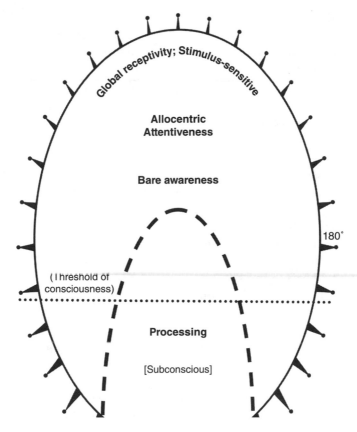

Global receptivity; Stimulus-sensitive

**Allocentric
Attentiveness**

Bare awareness

180°

(Threshold of
consciousness)

Processing

[Subconscious]

**Figure 7 A visual representation of bottom-up attentive processing,
on a background of bare awareness**

A global receptivity is being deployed. The sensitivities of countless receptors (black dots) are attuned to detect stimulus events that might
arrive unexpectedly from anywhere in the environment (externally or
internally). The more selfless the person, the more unalloyed can be the
resulting allocentric processing. Whereas such potential stimuli do register briefly in conscious awareness, much subconscious processing also
occurs subliminally, below the threshold of consciousness. Our vision is
limited to the frontal plane, from 0° on the left to 180° on the right.
Our hearing detects stimuli over a 360° range.

particular qualities of awareness to emerge spontaneously [ZB: 615–616]. Indeed, this condition of mental silence then evolves gradually—*by itself*—into an "extremely direct, keen and penetrating" degree of enhanced awareness. Along the way, many of the meditator's personal thoughts of Self will tend to drop off, as will conceptual barriers that had once served to separate the Self inside from the environment outside.

What kinds of advanced experiences result from this practice of "just sitting" (silent illumination)? Sheng-yen cites instructive metaphoric descriptions made by other persons.[13] Two cool autumn images originated with Ch'an Master Hongchi Zhengjue (1091–1157). In one, the setting was a cool, crisp day. At this time, the sky was "so high and clear that one can see the birds gliding gently high up in the blue." The other autumn scenery was a nocturne. Now the image was of a moon. This moon was shining so clearly in the sky that "everything in the land is illuminated by its cool and gentle light."

Neither description would suggest a master meditator who had always been looking down at the floor or at the ground. They do point to the fruits of a style of no-thought meditation (*wu-shin* in Chinese) that has become free of the discursive antics of the monkey mind. This kind of clear, calm mental field, during its earlier phases, becomes more open to receive—without judgment—whatever might enter from the spatial environment. In its later more objective phases, brief states of cooly illuminating insight can then emerge spontaneously [ZBR: 436]. These silent illumination techniques offer a sharp contrast to the more intensive techniques of top-down concentration that focus one's physical and psychic Self on a discrete task with deliberate goals in mind. Despite their blissful warmer overtones, these absorptions lack transformative powers [ZB: 471–479].

Background III: Optional Positions of Attention and Gaze: Up, or Down

Meditators who attended Nanrei Kobori-Roshi's subsequent retreats discovered that some of his standard meditation instructions could evolve.[14] One approach was first to look slowly and softly. Later the trainees were instructed to then "really, *really*" sustain a focus on something "outside yourself."[15] "Out there" is a key operative phrase in other-centered practices.

The trainees' next instruction was to let their eyelids close halfway and then to "shift your concentration to a point just above your eyes, between your eyebrows." It is important to notice that this was to be a *gentle* shift in attention. The shift was not intended to require effort. Instead, it was to remain "very simple: all you are doing is shifting your 'presence of mind,' your 'awareness' while you're 'focusing,' from *outside* to *inside* . . .".

The next instruction was to then let this relaxed awareness "sink down very slowly inside your Self, bringing your awareness back up between your eyebrows, then letting it sink down again." These suggestions are designed to enlist one's imagination, to switch between soft focusing and intense focusing, between outside and inside, between directing attention up and down. The trainees are being encouraged to wield attention *flexibly*, as if it were an instrument [ZB: 69–71]. In short, they're invited to be flexible, to experiment with different *simple* options, to discover which attentive approach works best for them. They are *not* being encouraged to conjure up visions or esoteric concepts.

Obviously, as soon as you lower your upper *eyelids*, these overhanging lids begin to block your upper fields of vision. The upper fields of vision are the fields blocked even more when your *eyes* also drift upward in the direction toward your *eyebrows*. Perhaps these related words (eyelids/ eyes/eyebrows) sound vaguely confusing. If so, please reread these sentences. Then *learn through simple direct experience*—the method that is the essence of Zen. Partially close your upper *eyelids*, gently elevate the gaze position of your *eyes*, and gaze up toward your *eyebrows* and beyond into your darkened upper fields of vision.

Background IV: Bodhidharma

The chapters in parts II and III have been suggesting a rationale for adding something to your later meditative repertoire: a slow, gentle drift of the eyes that results in gazing upward and farther outward. A particular statue of Bodhidharma happens to show this upward gaze position. It was carved out of wood in the late twentieth century. A brief explanation is in order.

Traditional accounts name Bodhidharma as the Indian monk who carried the meditation school of Buddhism into China and established it there during the sixth century. Therefore he is regarded as the first Zen patriarch in China. One legend suggests that Bodhidharma chose a unique way to avoid becoming drowsy while he was meditating. It was to cast off his two upper (drooping) eyelids and his two lower eyelids. Let us suspend disbelief temporarily, leaving us free to regard such an imaginary eyelid-ectomy solely as a vehicle for our own instruction. Then even this dramatic tall tale turns out to convey several points of useful information:

1. Now all available light could enter his eyes. These light energies could help him stay awake during the nine years (!) he was said to have spent meditating.

- **Raise your eyelids when you feel drowsy and allow more light to stimulate your brain.**
  If three-quarters down makes you drowsy, don't lower your eyelids so far. Adjust your eyelid level to your level of arousal.

  2. How did tea plants get started in China (where tea's stimulating properties could help monks stay awake during long hours of meditation)? The Bodhidharma legends go on to invent an even more imaginative explanation: it would be in the soil where his eyelids fell that the very first tea plants in China were said to have taken root and grown.

- **Use tea or coffee judiciously.**
  Too much caffeine causes too many mental and physical side effects.

  3. The symbolic act of casting off such vital parts of his body would further establish Bodhidharma as an ultraconscientious meditator. It helped to exemplify the dedication and seriousness of purpose of this new Ch'an school of meditation in China [SI: 202].

- **Be conscientious about your meditative practice, but follow the Buddha's more practical Middle Way, not the legendary excessive zeal associated with Bodhidharma.**

  4. This wide-eyed legend then gave rise to a further artistic convention: subsequent generations of artists began to depict Bodhidharma as lacking all four eyelids. Why does such an artistic custom become relevant to our present discussion? Because now when we look closely at one of Bodhidharma's many images, we usually can easily see the gaze position of his eyeballs. (In such

varied ways can mythology, art, and historical fiction converge to help readers remember certain aspects of neurophysiology.)

Consider the case in point, this statue in the author's possession.[16] The Japanese artist carved this 12-inch wooden statue with great skill. Especially noteworthy is the way he painted Bodhidharma's black pupils to render the gaze position of his eyes. They depict the monk's eyes as directed *upward*, at an angle of 45 degrees. There we observe that both eyes are deviated slightly to the left, and held parallel in the position of conjugate gaze. He is shown looking off into the distance.

Master Hakuin (1689–1769) was an outstanding Rinzai master. One of his available portraits shows Bodhidharma looking up and to the left.[17] Omori Sogen (1904–1994) was a recent Rinzai master, calligrapher, and artist. One of his paintings also depicts Bodhidharma gazing up and to the left.[18]

Another monk's eyes are deviated to an even greater degree: upward and to the left. This polychrome statue is often on exhibit in the Seattle Asian Art Museum. It has an explicit title: Monk at the Moment of Enlightenment. How did that Yuan Dynasty artist, seven centuries ago, depict an ordinary Buddhist monk at the moment that he entered the equivalent of *kensho-satori*? As turning to look far up and out to his left [SI: 116].

Background V: Relevant Examples from Tibetan Buddhism

The *Mahamudra* is a collection of ancient Buddhist teachings that are still practiced within the Kagyu order of Tibetan Buddhism.[19] Legends attribute their origins to a great Indian saint, Saraha. After he transmitted the teachings to Nagarjuna in the second or third century c.e., they eventually reached Tibet. (Some regard them as resembling a kind of "Tibetan Zen.") The teachings draw a clear distinction between (1) the superficial absorptions that can arise in the meditator who begins the Path of tranquillity and concentration (*shamatha*) and (2) the sudden transformations by insight (*prajna*) that occur during the more advanced states of awakening. In Zen, these are the later states of insight-wisdom referred to as *kensho* or *satori*.

On this latter path toward insight-wisdom, the Tibetan text specifies that the eyes are to be kept "wide open," watching, looking straight ahead. This manner of gazing is said to be similar to the techniques used to reveal the inherent *self-lessness* of the psyche. Moreover, meditators are advised to analyze very carefully the origins of each of their mental phenomena. How carefully? How persistent and discriminating are they expected to be when they pursue this introspective examination? Like "an inquisitive person crushing a bone with a stone!" This is not a formula for a nonthinking mind. It implies a rigorous analysis of the Self in the world. Indeed, the Dalai Lama once said: "For me, analytical meditation is most helpful" [SI: 153–154].

Highly adept Tibetan meditators also engage in a separate practice of "sky gazing." They approach this practice gradually while learning how to cultivate a stable form of receptive, intensified, "open presence awareness." The phrase is useful because it also suggests an open *presence of mind* (chapter 11).

The technique of "open presence" is not easily mastered because great subtleties abound in such a complex practice.[20] These adept meditators are deliberately choosing, at first, to direct their open eyes slightly upward toward empty, cloudless space. At the same time they are still trying to maintain an empty mind that remains open to realize the unity of awareness within this matrix of space. *Rigpa* is a term used in the Dzogchen tradition. It refers to an advanced state of consciousness devoid of all concepts, a state regarded as exemplifying the "unity of emptiness and cognizance."[21] It is said to represent a particular "knowing" of unconstructed space at this deepest experiential level.

Yongey Mingyur Rinpoche recently described this open setting. It was included in the way he learned about the Mahamudra (Dzogchen) Path from his father, a celebrated teacher in the Karma Kagyu school of Tibetan Buddhism.[22] His father would "simply sit in front of the large window and gaze off into the sky" above the Kathmandu Valley. Pointing out through the window, he advised his son: "Look out into the blue sky. Pure awareness is like space, boundless and open. It's always here. You don't have to make it up. All you have to do is rest in that."

Background VI: Gazing Up Involuntarily

Notice that a meditator might begin to employ such a Tibetan technique of sky gazing in either of two different ways: (1) in the sense of voluntarily gazing in "real time" up into the actual sky or (2) while exercising a vivid imagination in the course of an intense, virtual "re-visualization." On the other hand, it is essential to recognize that a relaxed practice is described in the earlier pages of this chapter. It is different. It is designed *ultimately* to help cultivate casual, random moments. *During these a meditator might happen to gaze up involuntarily.*

However semivolitionally one's eyes may be allowed to drift up during this meditative practice at first, the much later development of an involuntary movement takes on a very different significance. *Involuntary* gaze refers instead to a particular, momentary, reflexive act. It is what "happens" when we naturally glance upward either casually or in reaction to a random, unexpected stimulus. Why—under rare, yet propitious conditions—might such a seemingly trivial glance become of *causal* significance? Because it could retain the potential to contribute to the several sensorimotor mechanisms that happen to converge and trigger kensho. Sometimes chance coincidences cohere.

Language presents an interesting coincidence with regard to the emphasis on the allocentric, upper field, and upward gaze themes in this book. The Sino-Japanese word for "sky" is the same as the central Mahayana Buddhist term for "emptiness"[23] [ZB: 570–572; ZBR: 383–386]. The ideogram for emptiness is illustrated on the jacket cover of this book, a gift of semicursive calligraphy from Tanchu Terayama.

Shabkar (1781–1851) was an enlightened sage in the Tibetan tradition. His words provide an explicit testimony of a peak experience.[24] This state of consciousness might happen to a monk who not only lives where high, white mountain peaks invite people to look up casually into the sky, but whose own previous practices could also include gazing upward.[25] He specifies that delusions have vanished (the sky contains no clouds). Moreover, such an awakening is liberated from all prior bondage of the Self (this unlimited freedom retains no Self back in its center).

> I raised my head, looking up
> And saw the cloudless sky.
> I thought of absolute space, free from limits,
> . . . Then experienced a freedom
> Without center, without end.

11

Meanwhile, What Does "Being Mindful" Include?

> Mindfulness is not about "not feeling" or becoming detached from affect. . . . It is rather seeing something *as* it is, without further elaboration . . . seeing thoughts *as* mental events . . . rather than seeing them as having meaning for the integrity of self.
>
> J. Mark Williams[1]

> If your mind is fixed on a certain spot, it will be seized by that spot and no activities can be performed efficiently. Not to fix your mind anywhere is essential. Not fixed anywhere, the mind is everywhere.
>
> Zen Master Takuan (Soho) (1573–1645)[2]

Chapters 2 and 7 began to introduce mindfulness as a "family" of related practices [SI: 8–13]. At its operational core is a particular *quality and degree* of bare, dispassionate, nonreactive awareness. This awareness remains open to receive and register the immediacy of each successive event in *just this* present moment [ZB: 125–129].

Then, as the long meditative Path cultivates *both* top-down and bottom-up attention, attentiveness evolves from this basic core of short-term functions linked with one's working memory. Gradually, attentiveness develops an increasingly close association with a cluster of other significant attributes. Among these allies are subtle *overview functions*. These have access to *longer-term* associations.

One purpose of this chapter is to clarify how such a medley of short-term *and* long-term overview operations substantially expands the scope of mindfulness. Indeed, these dual overview functions are both sufficiently reflexive

Table 2
Dimensions of Re-mindfulness

	Links with Short-Term Working Memory	Links with Long-Term Memories, Incubated and Applied More Intuitively
General orientation	Toward goal-oriented conscious acts	Toward larger intuitive "big picture" issues
Usual time frame	Seconds to minutes	Variable; seconds to lifelong
Topic areas	Tactics of immediate, explicit relevance	Strategies and implicit policies of general significance
Mode of attention	More top-down for close monitoring	More bottom-up for the broad (meta-)overview
Quality of "presence of mind"	Active, focused on the immediate task	More passive, flexible, openly receptive to whatever might happen
Cues	Ongoing, anticipated	Inconstant, tangential, of random occurrence
Self-participation	More Self-centered	Openly other-centered
Examples	Numbering each breath; seeing individual trees	Kindness, compassion; seeing whole forests
Cultivated more by	Concentrative meditation	Receptive meditation

to meet the urgent tactical needs of our short-term working memory tasks and sufficiently "intelligent" to respond to our subtler long-term policy needs. The most important of these policy needs is for the evolution of compassion. Because this advanced degree of compassion (*karuna*) is so authentically selfless, it can respond with wisdom and skill to *any* event in the overall "big picture" [ZB: 648–653]. Table 2 begins to encompass the dimensions of this functional continuum.

Both time frames involve a quality often described as "presence of mind." Where is the mind "present"? *Both in the foreground of consciousness and in the subconscious background* of our deepest attitudes. Throughout its presence, such a "mind" has close affiliations with the old Pali term *sati*, as will be described later. Among these links are our basic memory functions. They enable us to recollect, retrieve, and reunite our associations. The monitoring functions that oversee our short-term memory at the nether end of this spectrum are reminiscent of the way a wavy red line appears instantly under a word, on a computer screen. It signals that the spell-checking function has just detected another mistake.

In contrast, off toward the long-term end of the overview spectrum, the scope of presence of mind includes the attributes of attitudes that have existed offstage (not just behind the curtain) for much longer intervals. These are our covert *subconscious* capacities. They can tap into larger ambient, cognitive issues that reflect our character traits and the way we judge cultural norms. These involve wide-looping association networks. Some could have been incubating data and integrating it loosely for decades. Their capacities enable us to automatically integrate long-term complex memory associations during intuitive leaps that are global, abstract, and far-sighted [SI: 202–211].

- **Notice that cultivating attentiveness to such a totally inclusive presence of mind would leave no extra room around any of its edges for absent-minded lapses to occur.**

Originally T. Rhys-Davids translated the Pali word *sati* as "mindfulness."[3] Thereafter, although this seemingly simple English word settled in to a secure place in Buddhist psychology,[4] its complex ingredients have resisted being disentangled and defined in precise neuroimaging terms. As Richard Davidson recently observed, substantial semantic and physiological issues arise in this field because, not only do the experimental conditions of measurement themselves involve emotional variables, but state and trait changes have also been taking place in the meditator's brain over time.[5]

Meanwhile, the elastic qualities of *sati* still allow this word to play a leading role in interpreting the basic meditation teachings of the *Sati*patthana Sutra.[6] The interpretations begin with the way *sati* is related to the verb *sarati*, "to remember." It implies "that which facilitates and enables memory."

Yet, sati's major assignment begins not just when we first register an event mindfully, and not when we then engage in an ordinary short-term serial working memory task like counting the number of breaths from one to ten. Its special role extends "to bring this moment back to mind at a later time."[7] Note that "later" can mean *much* later. Indeed, it can mean decades later—at a time when our net of attentive processing might *cast itself intuitively* to retrieve abstract configurations, coded much earlier in covert functions that had been elaborated upon further during incubation at subconscious levels. (Chapter 20 provides one example) Viewed in this context, sati would represent the *involuntary*, broadly based, *supraordinate* networking functions that could facilitate insight.

Clearly, no attentive focus that remains narrowly targeted on short-term working memory describes such an expansive breadth of mind. Indeed, once the early Buddhists had identified the key "awakening factors" that enabled advanced states of insight to arise, how did they then view this particular aspect of the term *sati*? They regarded it as both the foundation and *the* most prominent prerequisite among all the mental components that converged when a person became enlightened.

For contemporary meditators, two points are crucially important to appreciate: (1) these "intelligent," *re-mindful* surveillance and overview functions have the capacity to operate *involuntarily* and (2) a *balanced* program of selfless meditative training serves to cultivate their continuum of short-term *and* long-term attributes.

Why must such a training program be increasingly *selfless*? Because "an aloof quality of uninvolved detached observation" remains at the core of sati.[8] This basic aspect of sati is similar to that of a *clear, objective, choiceless, awareness* (table 1). This unattached perspective enables its objective observer to remain impartially aware of events, beyond any immediate temptation to actively interfere with them. Freud once described this calm, quiet attentiveness as an "evenly hovering attention" [ZB: 125–129]. Accurate, objective diagnosis is the essential prelude to any form of effective therapy.

Clearly, a spectrum of functional sequences seems involved within the several re-mindful aspects of sati. Some begin during the first milliseconds of preattention that correspond with bare attention (as shown in figure 1) (in Pali, *manasikara*) [SI: 229]. Thereafter, as table 2 indicates, their further, substantial refinements might seem to represent the global expansion and temporal extension of an overview (meta-) attentiveness. This can be cultivated during receptive meditation practices that are poised increasingly to enlist the bottom-up forms of attention in particular (figure 7).

At this far end of our continuum of memory, the contrasts between sati and samadhi's sharply focused concentrated attention become even more evident. Analayo comments that the Pali literature tends to interpret *samadhi* as both an enhancement of our *selective*, top-down mental functions and as a *narrowing* of our breadth of attention. In contrast, sati serves more to enhance our general memory retrieval functions and to *expand* our breadths of attention.[9]

You keep emphasizing the need for a balanced attentiveness. How can I maintain this optimum balance between concentrative and receptive meditative techniques?

To begin with, your brain's innate capacities can already alternate flexibly and autonomously throughout this continuum (chapter 5). With regard to meditation, the Buddha explained that the proper balance of effort on the Path is the "Middle Way." Choosing a musical analogy, he compared it with the fine-tuning adjustments that one makes when one tunes the strings of a lute—the strings are stretched neither too tightly nor too loosely[10] [ZB: 235–240].

Empirical observation suggests the value of this Middle Way. When a person's conservative meditative practices do cultivate a fine-tuned spectrum of *balanced* attentive capacities, their complementary assets help sponsor a series of little insights. These are "little openings." Collectively, they help resolve a wide variety of life's simpler everyday issues of working memory. Less often, other openings tap into dimensions that address overall policies and major strategies. They illuminate deeper, existential topics that involve matters of career choices, lifelong relationships, and death.

As this continuum of capacities linked with ongoing mindful practices gradually evolves, its priorities develop along lines that become increasingly *intuitive*. On some occasions, the meditator's bare awareness might turn spontaneously into a more or less anonymous *out*flowing of appreciation: a moment focused keenly on Just This event in the natural world outside (chapter 8). At other times of mindful introspection, the meditator's awareness could be turning far inside, into long moments of coolly objective, unsparing Self-analysis. In this inner world, a still, small conscience keeps wondering: Who *are* you, *really*? And keeps probing: Which of your native abilities will serve life most appropriately in the few years remaining [ZBR: 352–354]? None of these stern, silent probings represent a careless, short-sighted, no-minded approach to living. None can support a mission in life that remains ignorant, uncaring, or unethical.

To summarize thus far, when sati is interpreted liberally, its breadth and elasticity can (1) describe the ethical *right* mindfulness inherent throughout the noble eightfold Path (the term *samma sati* is applicable in this instance) and (2) accommodate a broad spectrum of overview capacities.

In a meditative context, we might refer to such properties as *"re-mindfulness."* Standard dictionaries do not list this word, yet the continuum of a meditator's presence of mind depends on the everyday training of such vital, automatic *re*-mindfulness functions.[11]

Well, O.K., being mindful is more complicated than I thought. Still, how might I begin its practice indoors, on the cushion?

- **Remain aware of whatever happens in just this present moment.**

  Begin by registering these percepts, thoughts, and emotions at the level of bare awareness. Colors, luminosities, and shifting densities may arise in the dark vacancy under your partially closed eyelids. Observe them with detachment. They come and go. Continue to listen all around, while still noticing the faint movements down in your lower abdomen that are linked with breathing in and out. The first part of an openly receptive mental landscape begins with just noticing *what* happens. Just the simplest things — the internal and external visual scene, faint breathing movements, and the global auditory environment. *What* is happening?

- **Become a barometer, observing your own "inner weather," noticing how your arousal state, alertness, and emotions vary up and down.**

  Become so keenly aware of the way your consciousness varies its form, content, and turbulence that you can reliably identify and almost predict your own emotions. The spectrum of consciousness fluctuates substantially during the 24 hours of a day. Each transient shift demonstrates the essential impermanence (*annica*) inherent in our ever-changing cycles of existence [ZB: 338–347; SI: 246–247].

Something else can happen on the cushion when mindful introspection surveys the landscape of your consciousness. Occasionally, a fresh wave of arousal or alertness might surge spontaneously into your current level of bare awareness [ZB: 457–460]. As this arousal wave crests, you can experience the whole field of visual and auditory attention opening wider. An enhanced sense of mental and perceptual clarity can accompany this involuntary opening. During these moments, at the same time that your eyelids open up wider and your peripheral fields of external vision expand in every direction, your gaze may also tend to drift upward.

- **Accept with patience what might at first seem to be your limitations.**
  Remember that every mind wanders. Subtle *re-mindful* orientations operate *subconsciously*. It takes a very long time for their trait skills to be fully developed. Gradually, *they* learn how to shift *"our"* mental sets. Remember: *It is not "our doing" that causes these involuntary re-mindful shifts to be operating. It is in their grace that attention returns to its prior focus.* On occasion, these intuitive mechanisms will also evolve into little "openings", the casting of a net of free associations that coalesce into a novel state of insightful comprehension (chapter 18). Meanwhile, just be patient with your seemingly glacial pace of progress.[12]

Your Self-correcting brain will continue to train *itself* during months and years of repetition. First, it will learn how to recognize *and* how to correct for the fact that it had just been straying. Later, its introspective probings begin to realize, intuitively, which personality traits are the underlying cause of your recurrent long-range existential dilemmas. Back when you were a child, without constantly having to think about it, you gradually learned how to balance and steer a bicycle. Then, too, you were aided by a continuum of similarly subconscious "intelligent," procedural memory skills. It was only by this direct seat-of-the-pants and handlebar experience that you learned how to ride a bicycle, not by reading about it.

Yes, I remember when I first learned how to ride a bike. But how can just sitting quietly and meditating cultivate any such "neuroplastic" learning process?

Background I: Brain Training in the Course of Direct Experience

The previous two chapters outlined how the training program begins. First, both brain and body start to attend to a few immediate tasks. Then—even without your overt prompting—you'll discover how a gentle, effortless, bottom-up, reflexive, habitual act of *re-mindfulness* starts to return attention back to its original focus [SI: 21–26].

Next comes the hard part. It is also the most enduring and most practical part of the training. It begins only when you start to directly apply what your brain is learning on the cushion to the emotional vicissitudes in your daily life practice (Japanese: *shugyo*) (part V). Did you first learn how to ride using a bicycle that had training wheels? If so, you know you later had to take off those wheels in order to navigate the uneven terrain that lay ahead. . . .

Maybe so, yet how do we know that when you "neural Buddhists" proclaim the merits of some Asian style of meditation, the conclusions aren't warped by your own subconscious biases?

You don't. However the term *neuroplasticity* is a recent buzzword. It refers to a long list of subtle changes that transform *any* brain whenever it "learns" something. This happens whether or not its consciousness "knows" that it's being "trained" [ZB: 223–228]. Suppose you were an adult monkey now being trained to learn a special new skill. Your goal is to assemble the separate parts that will become a long-handled rake. You'll need to use this rake to reach a slice of apple far beyond an arm's reach. Your brain develops the new connections it needs for this novel task after only two weeks of regular practice [ZBR: 150–152].

It turns out that the connections in a real monkey's newly trained brain are highly relevant to how we meditators train our attentive processing. Notably, the real monkey's new connections bridge a crucial gap. They link the intraparietal sulcus (iPS) of the upper stream with the temporo-parietal junction (TPJ) down below (figures 2 and 4). Our primate relatives are sending us a message: adopt a balanced approach when learning a new skill [SI: 258–259].

Human brains also change when they engage in a course of visual training. Recent fMRI evidence confirms that neuroplasticity develops over several days when humans repeatedly practice a visual learning task.[13] Lewis and colleagues studied fourteen human subjects while they were being trained to attend to a single target: an inverted letter T (⊥).[13] It was located down in their *left* lower visual field. As this left lower stimulus task became progressively more familiar, the subjects gradually reduced the corresponding fMRI responses of their opposite *right* dorsal visual cortex. During this learning process, progressively less deactivation also took place in their medial frontal and parietal "attention-off" regions (elsewhere often referred to as default regions, referable here more to our Self-other continuum).

Later, the subjects' spontaneous functional MRI connectivities were retested while they were once again back in a resting state. The data revealed that these slow, intrinsic, resting-state functional connectivities had also changed in complex ways that could be attributable to the subjects' prior training. Thus, when the attentive processing that enters into our visual learning is repeatedly applied to one particular visual quadrant, it seems to "sculpture" the basic intrinsic patterns of spontaneous cortical connectivity that link the brain's networks together.

The subjects' first-person reports revealed another noteworthy result of this training. They began to see the inverted T target "effortlessly." The target seemed to be "popping out" into the foreground from the background. "Pop-out" reports suggest that the training had also enhanced the subjects' preattentive processing. How? By engaging their multiple, subconscious, subcortical pathways of fast parallel processing [ZB: 278–281; ZBR: 175–176; SI: 28–29, 35–36].

It remains to be determined how a trained meditator's distant networks might respond to the potential release of bombesin-like peptides from the large von Economo nerve cells in the anterior cingulate and fronto-insular regions[14] [ZBR: 84; SI: 138–139; 238–239].

12

How Can Brain Research Help Us Understand Mindful Meditation?

Finally, research is beginning to prove what mindfulness practitioners have known for centuries . . . that greater attention, awareness, acceptance, and compassion can facilitate more flexible, adaptive responses to stress, which, in turn, can help free us from suffering and realize greater health and well being.

J. Greeson[1]

Our era is increasingly aware that its technical sophistications can break down. Therefore the fact that Greeson also refers to mindfulness itself as an "inner technology" helps one anticipate that attempts to find all the neuroimaging correlates of mindfulness could become complicated [ZBR: 214–226; SI: 35–47, 98–103]. Baerensten and colleagues also reviewed the mindfulness literature in 2009. They concluded that while most such reports were "still somewhat contradictory and variable," the data did tend to point in one direction: toward activations in brain areas "that are related to the regulation of attention."[2] Daito Kokushi would have concurred.

However, this review by Baerentsen and colleagues also underlined an import point: the need to find what causes "stability." Perceptual stability refers to our span of attention. It inquires: How *long* can we hold our focus consistently on one task? But our *emotional* stability is also important. One index of emotional stability is sufficient resilience to maintain a demeanor of cheerfulness. This stable, positive attitude, together with a basic simplicity, helps us identify which sage person has become free from the cognitive tangles, rigid opinions, anger, and other emotional swings caused by their prior overconditioning. Because even when such liberated individuals confront stressful circumstances, their smiling countenance and other body language then identify them as resilient beings farther along on the Path toward the stage of ongoing enlightened traits [ZB: 413–419, 637–645; ZBR: 242, 397–398].

In Japan, despite having a round base, the eight-inch toy Bodhidharma conveys this message, because it is heavily weighted below. Children learn that despite any attempt to knock him over. Bodhidharma always rolls back quickly into an upright posture. As the saying goes, "Seven times down, eight times *up!*"

How does a program of balanced long-term meditation transform a three-pound human brain and enable it to become more receptive and stable? How could meditation simultaneously not only enhance the inherent stability we need for our best sensorimotor performance, but also reduce the variability caused by uncontrolled emotions? Simple sports metaphors help ground such wordy conceptual issues in tangible actions [ZB: 668–677]. Choosing a skiing metaphor, Baerentsen and colleagues cite a familiar distinction: the beginning skier who wobbles and falls; the advanced skier who cruises downhill with seemingly impossible grace.

And, speaking of basic concepts, why would a normal brain have evolved a *slow* cycle of spontaneous, reciprocal, low-amplitude, fluctuating activations and deactivations (chapters 2, 3, and 5)? These intrinsic patterns shift back and forth only several times a *minute* between our Self-referential networks and our external attention networks [SI: 103–108]. A tennis metaphor may help us understand why. Observe how top professional tennis players behave when they are about to receive a serve. Poised in this alert receiving mode, we see them shifting their balance—back and forth—first toward one foot, then toward the other. They alternate sides. They never remain in one static, dead-center, flat-footed stance. Moreover, their angle of gaze is directed slightly upward, enabling them to react the instant they see the distant server's racquet strike the tossed ball. When the receivers insert this dynamic, reciprocal component into their behavioral equation, it seems to facilitate their next move, in a split second, toward wherever the serve might land [ZBR: 195].

It turns out that a recent study addressed this important point about how meditative practices can train the *stability* of attentiveness.[3] Lutz and colleagues reported the behavioral and electroencephalograph (EEG) results of a three-months' period of intensive meditative training. The meditators were practicing a mixture of top-down concentrative focusing techniques plus bottom-up receptive techniques [SI: 6–7]. The way they performed dichotic listening tasks indicated that their several practices during this retreat had increased their attentional stability. Moreover, their efficiencies also increased. At the end, they also required *lesser* degrees of cortical processing to meet the stringent demands of this auditory task.

The entire January issue of the journal *Emotion* began 2010 with a series of eight articles. Most authors had used neuroimaging techniques in an effort to help define and try to "capture" mindfulness as an independent variable. Although the contents of this whole special issue lie beyond our present scope, the introductory comments by J. Mark Williams,[4] plus the reflections on the contents of the issue by Richard Davidson[5] are recommended. Each provides a cogent review of this increasingly large area of recent research.

Williams's figure 2 becomes of interest with regard to the questions raised both in the title of this chapter and in the previous chapter: What Does Being Mindful Include? This figure diagrams one way a meditator could perform a mindfulness practice called the "body scan." It is a substantial task first to engage and then to disengage one's focus of attention fifty times, moving deliberately from one region of the body to another. The task requires the trainee to accomplish at least five things: (1) to hold on to short-term "meta-intentions in working memory"; (2) to closely monitor these successive scanning sites in order to notice when any mind-wandering occurs; (3) to disengage from each site or from incidental mind-wandering (thus invoking the "circuit-breaker" functions of the TPJ); (4) to return attention instantly to its intended focus; and (5) to simply maintain a benign background acknowledgment that such mind-wandering does occur, aided by an ongoing positive "attitude of friendly curiosity and compassion," while also suspending any attitude of "comparison, analysis or judgment."[6]

Given the instaneity and compound nature of these multiple activities, one can appreciate that many ingredients included in mindfulness could be difficult for researchers to isolate and capture with functional MRI per se. In addition, at least nine factors are identifiable within the longitudinal approach that leads meditators toward a gradual dissolution of their basic Self-centeredness [ZB: 141–145].

What do you mean by "instaneity"? Give some examples.

It takes around 200–300 milliseconds for our voluntary decisions to shift attention. This delay of 0.2–0.3 seconds has been referred to as "the clock speed of free will."[7] Recent EEG studies suggest that synchronized electrophysiological oscillations provide functional connections that link our medial prefrontal cortex with our occipital cortex.[8] The two regions constantly exchange information in both a top-down *and* bottom-up manner. Top-down synchronized coupling can occur between 500 and 1,400 milliseconds after a visual stimulus. Bottom-up sharing occurs even when the brain makes visual performance errors that the subject does not consciously recognize as erroneous.

In the smaller monkey brain, microelectrodes measure a *total* transmission time of only 5 milliseconds for the "hot-line" circuit that speeds visual impulses from the superior colliculus, on through their relay in the pulvinar of the thalamus, and then on up into the middle temporal area of the cortex.[9]

Speaking of complexity, although this book is entitled "Meditating Selflessly," you've barely hinted how some deeper brain regions might be involved in arriving at selflessness. So, again, what is it exactly about the mindful training of attention that could later enable our brain to cancel its basic Self-centeredness?

A brief commentary here is certainly in order to clarify the speed with which deeper mechanisms operate and the ways that a balanced program of mindfully training attention could set the stage for the much later arrival of selflessness (chapters 2 and 5).

Background: Deeper Origins of Selflessness

Events that can culminate in selflessness begin in the *subcortical* mechanisms of preattention. These come into play immediately, in the earliest milliseconds of our covert, hard-wired, most primitive forms of bottom-up attention. Following soon thereafter are top-down sequences descending from higher cortical levels. Meditation researchers in the future confront formidable technical challenges in the face of the millisecond immediacy and distributed nature of these physiological interactions. Their multidisciplinary research will need to answer more precisely the question just posed—in terms of sequences that evolve millisecond by millisecond. Given our contemporary state of ignorance, let us begin to rephrase this question as follows: By what deeper mechanisms can a stimulus that activates the sharp tip of our attentiveness, plus our more global receptivities, *and* the circuit-breaker functions of the TPJ, go on to precipitate a *deactivation* of our chiefly midline Self-referential fronto-parietal regions?

No answers will come easily, given the examples just cited of events that unfold in thousandths of a second and enter into the brain's web of oscillating interactivities.[10] By contrast, conventional functional MRI signal peaks are delayed for from *three to six seconds after* neuronal events occur. The good news is that magnetoencephalography (MEG) offers a way to localize *and* measure the coarse-grained (and literally bottom-up) visual information as it first speeds on up to, and through, its hard-wired gateways in our thalamus [SI: 19, 228–232]. For example, when this "distant early warning signal" is processed up in the orbital frontal gyrus, this part of the frontal lobe might help us reach a crude initial guess about *what* we see looming on our immediate event horizon. How soon do gamma-wave MEG signals reach their peak in this orbital frontal region? Within as few as 200 to 220 milliseconds after we glimpse an angry face for a mere three-tenths of a second.

An interesting point is that this early orbital frontal peak can develop such a "preview" 10 milliseconds *before* the amygdala develops its (limbic) peak, and 50–80 milliseconds *before* the fusiform gyrus develops its (visual) peak way down underneath the right temporal lobe. This MEG data suggest that a relatively *early* wave of orbital frontal feedback could already be poised to provide a tentative top-down cortical alert to our limbic system and could also be ready to enhance the more refined perceptual responses within our lower cortical visual pathways.[11]

So to return to the deep question and to rephrase it once again: Through which pathways do incoming sensory stimuli relay their *early* signals, which then converge on successive switching mechanisms down in the center of the brain? Because down *here* is where our major gates and deeper master switches exist. Regions along the axial center of the brain tend to be more primitive in terms of evolution. On the other hand, they are also in a central position to enable *both* hemispheres of our brain to shift, not simply from one foot to the other, but in a coherent manner that could ultimately help transform the way we respond during highly sophisticated socially adaptive behaviors.

In anticipation of such future research into the long meditative Path, why has it been plausible to envision a vitally important role for the thalamus and its reticular nucleus? Because the ongoing tone and selectivity of these deep nuclei normally modulate, not only our constructs of Self (chapter 5), but also govern our ordinary states of sleep and wakefulness, perceptual life, and everyday behavior (chapter 16).[12]

Events at excitatory synapses are rightfully emphasized in the nervous system. However, the *inhibitory* role of the *reticular nucleus* is crucial for two reasons: (1) Inhibition is poised to quench the fires of our unfruitful emotions down at their limbic relay through the thalamus. (2) The reticular nucleus can also influence a wide range of sensorimotor, cognitive, and state/trait functions. How? It can govern not only its own inhibitory GABA nerve cells, it can also influence the functions of a variety of other deep thalamic nuclei as they interact to regulate perception and states of consciousness [ZB: 263–274; ZBR: 167–179; SI: 87–94].

Yu and colleagues recently made a preclinical study of the deep auditory pathway.[13] They found responsive nerve cells in the reticular nucleus that were already twice as sensitive to novel auditory stimuli as were the auditory relay cells nearby in the medial geniculate nucleus of the thalamus. Some reticular nucleus cells also had an added capacity: they could inhibit their *own* neighboring reticular nerve cells! This *local* capacity for intrareticular disinhibition could enable medial geniculate nerve cells to react with an enhanced response to the signal of a novel auditory stimulus in a way that might further contribute to triggering a state of kensho.

Humans aren't unique. Both we and rats have a deep midline thalamic nucleus, the *nucleus reuniens*.[14] To this reuniens come massive contributions from the medial prefrontal cortex. From it relay vital messages that go on to inform both the hippocampal formation and the upper parietal cortex. This circuit then loops back to the orbitomedial frontal cortex [ZBR: 172]. Was this reuniens nucleus well-named? If so, then such an ancient pathway might help link our coded engrams into a widely distributed network of remindful configurations. These could quickly reunify many useful disparate associations of our short-term and/or long-term, intuitive memory functions (table 2). Consciousness would never be aware of the deep resources of this information until it surfaced.

Intricate circuitries also interconnect our frontal lobes [ZBR: 158–167], thalamus [ZBR: 167], and basal ganglia [ZB: 197–201, 675–677; SI: 205–207]. Acting in concert, they enable large portions of our brain to operate "intelligently," involuntarily, subconsciously, and with high degrees of reflexive autonomy (chapter 18). Our lives depend on such "automatic pilots." With great skill their hidden assets co-manage our Self-correcting attributes. When their soft, coded voices inform our lowly listening, we're guided in the tacit directions toward virtues that we sometimes call our "better Selves."[15]

Each human brain contains multiple arrays of similar looping circuits. Their connections provide important routes through which our overview networks can access subconscious levels, enabling us to automatically draw upon vast data resources from past experience. Consulting these, we shape our immediate responses to meet the short-term needs *and* long-range implications of the present moment.

How can so much of our seeing, and hearing, begin not only preattentively, but also remain *below* our threshold of consciousness [ZB: 278–281; ZBR: 179–183]? Parallel processing through multiple networks provides a plausible explanation. Networks that could skillfully anticipate forthcoming events had survival value in the past. Unfortunately, we've long outgrown the need for their many rigid expectations that place too Self-centered a "spin" on what we perceive. Now, any overemotionalized percept that hijacks our responses works too often to our disadvantage. By now, readers may appreciate why researchers could take such a long time to tease apart every subliminal circuit converging into the functions affiliated with the four-letter word *sati* (chapter 11).

Isn't there a simpler explanation for some of the other positive effects attributed to a decades-long program of balanced mindful meditative training?

Rephrasing the question again, could long-term training serve to enhance the *rate* of the normal processes that enable individual meditators to mature decade by decade? For example, could this occur by a series of subtle readjustments? Couldn't these improve the outworn patterns and synchronies of the functions oscillating among the thalamo-cortico-basal ganglia networks [SI: 114, 228–235, 237–244]? If research teams received appropriate funding for several decades, they could begin to recognize such a favorable influence. How? By the way the meditators' psychophysiological and neuroimaging profile diverged from that of the control group. Ultimately, this will involve studying individual meditators and controls multidimensionally for decades, aided by the latest neuroimaging and most sophisticated behavioral techniques. The working hypothesis would be that some meditating subjects would be on a trajectory of development showing that they had become increasingly simplified, stable, and compassionate and were poised to act skillfully. Other subjects, starting from their own baseline, would lag behind.

How might it be possible for a meditator to develop traits of buoyant resilience like a toy Bodhidharma—those deep attitudinal changes that reflect an extraordinary, stable, long-term tilt toward a positive emotional valence? Recent evidence from the Davidson team at the University of Wisconsin is noteworthy.[16] It suggests that our capacity to sustain such positive emotions involves connections that link the nucleus accumbens down in the ventral striatum with the left middle frontal gyrus up on the convexity of the cortex (mFG in figure 2).

Meanwhile, the theme of selflessness explored throughout these pages keeps pointing toward a complex profile of subtle interacting processes. They're not simple. No person can "achieve" such a result during an eight-week or three-month program, or "attain" enlightenment from a single peak experience.[17] Selflessness points back toward incremental transformations. These develop gradually, over decades, at cortical, subcortical, and brainstem levels. Over time, *they manifest themselves*. How? In the form of a present-moment ongoing awareness; in greater simplicity, stability, wisdom, and skillfully applied compassion. These attributes emerge involuntarily on the long Path toward the exceptional stage of ongoing enlightened traits [ZB: 637–653].

- **If you would begin to walk the endless Path toward such enlightened traits, then it is absolutely essential to strengthen your practice by going on a retreat.** The next chapter discusses why this is so.

Part IV

Attending Meditative Retreats

If you don't suffer hardship, you won't arrive at deep realization.

Ch'an Master Yuan-wu Kequin (1063–1135)

Why Go on a Retreat?

> When Heaven is about to confer a great office on you, it first exercises your mind with suffering and your sinews and bones with toil.
>
> Mencius (372–289 B.C.E.)

> The flowering of man's spiritual nature is as natural and strict a process of evolution as the opening of a rose or a morning glory. But there is this difference: while the plant must have a congenial environment . . . the human flowering often takes place amid the most adverse surroundings. . . .
>
> John Burroughs (1837–1921)

Many religious traditions hold periodic retreats. Ideally, the retreat is held where one can alternate between sitting meditation and walking outdoors in pleasant natural scenery. In the quiet environment of a retreat you have time to consolidate your practice, explore what makes you angry and dissatisfied, discover who you really are, and rededicate yourself to heeding the silent callings of authentic values that you deeply believe in.

Reading words on a page is an "armchair Zen" approach. That's O.K. But are you completely satisfied with your Self, the ways you relate to other persons, and your direction in life? Few are. One remedy is authentic meditative practice. Can Zen practice become such an agency of transformation, help you restructure dysfunctional traits? Yes, but only when first you set aside the time to identify what your problems are and then take the time to examine them objectively. A Zen meditative retreat offers the opportunity to do just this.

Decades ago it was more common to hear about rigorous "Outward Bound" programs that were usually conducted in a wilderness setting. Today, they are still intended to "foster personal growth and responsibility and to encourage the participants to reach beyond their limitations."[1] "Outward Bound" still implies that you confront the *internal* sources of your problems, and acknowledge that you resist change itself.

A rigorous retreat presents you with similar opportunities. In the course of being challenged physically and mentally, you can emerge inspired by a fresh sense of what you're capable of. Your body-mind will be learning a range of new skills and at levels much deeper than mere intellectual knowledge. As is the case with other procedural learning skills, these subtle residua tend to linger in the form of a quiet competence. It needs no pat on the back, nor does it expect one.

On a retreat, your body-mind will no longer be diverted into another noisy day of mindless multitasking. Instead of electronic distractions, you'll have the luxury of silent time. Soon you'll discover that Zen is a contact sport, not a spectator sport. During first-hand, direct *experiences* with the aches and pains that afflict your physical Self, you will relearn how much your emotional Self—your own resistances—is responsible for your suffering.

You will also meet other opinionated extensions of your psychic Self. In silence, for a change, you will ponder why you can't tolerate some persons, yet are attracted to others. These realizations arrive up close and personal [ZBR: 259]. They won't be distant abstractions, as are the second-hand psychopathologies that afflict characters in movies or in TV soap operas.

A Zen religious retreat is called a *"sesshin."* It literally means "to collect the mind." When you enter into a retreat, you become a team member in a web of interrelationships.

Having decided to share in the community responsibility of this support group, you make a more intensive effort than you would when you meditate at home by yourself. Longer retreats provide opportunities to discover who you are each time you confront, embrace, accept, knuckle under, and endure different aspects of mental and physical suffering [ZB: 230–232].

Life already seems like an obstacle course. Why should I subject myself to a rigorous retreat?

The Buddha condensed his basic message into one sentence: "Suffering I teach, and the way out of suffering." Going on a retreat commits you to reach out beyond simply viewing a spiritual path as an abstract concept. Once you undertake this personal plunge into direct experience and vote with your feet, you'll finally be assigning to your program of meditative training the top priority it deserves. Therefore,

- **Sign up for a retreat. Show up and stay the course.**
  Register for this retreat as naturally as you would consider taking your car in to be serviced at regular intervals. (This is your time to undergo a "body-mind tune-up," comparable to an oil, lube, and spark plug change.) Thereafter, you may actually discover that you (like your car) have been invigorated and are now running more efficiently. Start by signing up for a one-day retreat. Later, go off for a weekend retreat. Keep reaching out toward the edge of your comfort zone.

  Expect parts of your psyche and body to put up stiff resistance. It's been said that the only person who truly welcomes change is a baby with a wet diaper. Is meditation boring? Are you bothered by the expense, the aching muscles, the Self-imposed silence that stops you from talking? Examine all resistance.

- Probe by asking: What is this resistance? Who is resisting? Why?
- Prepare a solid mental and physical foundation before you go on a retreat.
  You must be in shape in order to meditate multiple times a day. Maintain sound commonsense hygienic practices. Prepare days in advance for the somatic and psychic stresses you will encounter. A calibrated training program provides the foundation. It allows you to remain calm, attentive, and to drop into extended moments of clear, mindful introspection throughout the retreat. Avoid any last-minute rush.

At home, increase the frequency and the length of your regular periods of meditation. Spend more time stretching and exercising the muscles of your back, neck, and abdomen. You're depending on these muscle groups to sustain an erect, alert posture. Practice sitting in different postures. These include kneeling, or sitting on the front half of a folding chair. It helps to have options whenever sitting erect on the cushion becomes too uncomfortable.

Sidestep the misguided appeals from any source that could entice you to take any mind-altering recreational drugs [ZB: 424–426; ZBR: 251–255; SI: 267–268].

- **Meditation, not medication.**
  Meditation is itself a mind-manifesting agency that leads to long-term character change. Psychedelics are counterproductive.
- **Work vigorously between meditation periods.**
  Physical exercise helps you maintain optimum levels of cardiorespiratory fitness even though you are sitting quietly and meditating several hours each day. Older adults who maintain higher levels of aerobic

fitness turn out to have larger hippocampal volumes and better spatial memories.[2] Basic yoga stretching exercises are recommended, especially on awakening. Lying flat on your back during the free intervals helps relieve the muscle aches associated with repeated erect sitting.

- **Pay close attention during walking meditation in order to become one with "Just Walking."**
  Just Walking is a fluid practice. It does not need to be synchronized with your breathing. Yet the pace is measured, neither too slow nor too fast. This gives you enough time to focus on the tactile and proprioceptive events that signal each contact your foot makes. Mindful walking attends both to the stepping forward and to the feel of the heel and ball of the foot as they each meet the floor or ground. Mindful walking means that you extend the same top-down meditative mode into walking that permeates the basic way you sit zazen. This is not easy. You are temporarily setting aside a whole lifetime of casual automatic gait and mind-wandering habits.

The Rinzai Zen style of walking meditation often proceeds at a faster pace. However, a slower pace has this distinct advantage: as soon as your mind wanders, you are reminded because your foot then veers off course, and you now have the direct experience of becoming slightly unbalanced.[3] During lengthy retreats, the intervals of walking meditation provide a welcome dynamic change, relieving muscles and joints that have begun to ache from sitting quietly in one position.

Free periods of outdoor walking meditation are not conducted in the usual single file. They allow you to meander and linger at your own pace and to openly engage in various random moments of cloud-watching, bird-watching, and observing Nature in general.

Isn't group meditation supposed to encourage a sense of community? Most of these suggestions still sound like I would be withdrawn, focusing on my own navel, not communicating with other people.

- **Relearn the profound merits of solitude.**
  Indeed, the root origins of the word *monk* refer to a solitary person. Why will you be cautioned on silent retreats not to speak and not to look at other people? These caveats are designed to help everyone settle down. You're spared from the standard social overtures that distract you into trivial conversations.[4] Incidentally, silent retreats also free you from hearing the Self-reinforcing sounds of your own vocalizations.

  The practice of solitude is only a temporary withdrawal. At the close of the silent retreat, you will then share in the warmth of more fruitful social interactions, renewing your sense of community with old and new friends at a more appropriate time. But until then:

- **Maintain your practice of silence.**
  It's a rare privilege. Extended silence takes on remarkable powers. It enables you to hear the still, small voice that otherwise languishes lowly within. Quiet acts as a universal solvent [ZB: 633–636]. Silence on retreats becomes part of the prelude toward that distant state which Master Huang-po had once described as the "stillness beyond all activity." He was pointing toward a particular interval of deep, prolonged mental clarity. At this moment, one's usual Self-referential mind drops off and conscious-

ness becomes totally free from all the cluttered thought streams that were full of wordy concepts and discriminations.

- **Avoid mirrors.**
A retreat helps you exercise other forms of visual restraint. Refrain from looking at your face either in a mirror or when you might see it reflected in a window or on the surface of water. By not looking at your own face and hair, you avoid reinforcing your usual *I-Me-Mine*-centered Self-image. (Keep asking: *Who needs to look?*)

The Path of Zen training offers no soft cloth for polishing the mirror of this Self-image. Retreats offer something more akin to coarse sandpaper. It proves useful when rounding off each sharp opinion that we soon discover projecting from our personality. After many retreats, if we're especially fortunate, perhaps the "sword of Manjusuri" might arrive. The phrase refers to that mythical bodhisattva whose sharp sword of insight-wisdom briefly severs the roots of Selfhood during a major peak experience [ZB: 137–145, 545–549; ZBR: 37–40; SI: 201–202] (chapter 21).

Are you suggesting that both regular daily-life practice and periodic retreats might somehow help me access this rare state of consciousness? And that inside this state, I might become free from my egocentricities and be graced by other deep insights as well?

That's the general idea. Siddhartha is an exemplar. However, any such suggestion is subject to countless qualifications. For example:

* **Don't think that you can become 100% "enlightened" by one brief awakening experience. Any first awakening serves merely as the beginning of the training** [ZBR: 394–398].

During the next decades of your daily life practice, much further "sanding" will be needed to smooth off all the multiple rough edges that you had developed earlier. And multiple cuttings-off of the deep roots of Self are also required in order to realize every potential source of transformation.

Consider the teachings: Siddhartha had spent at least *six* prior years of rigorous searching for the truth before he became supremely enlightened under the Bodhi tree. The concluding sections of his Satipatthana Sutra hinted that it might take a minimum of *seven years or so* for a substantial realization to occur.[5] He also specified certain preconditions to be followed by a person who wished to develop the requisite qualities of wisdom. We discuss these further in part V.

I've heard that you wake up at some ungodly hour during Zen retreats and lose sleep. Won't I get drowsy and tend to nod off while trying to meditate?

You probably will at first. The early morning rising and other measures are designed to introduce a calibrated degree of stress responses into the retreat setting. However, waking up before dawn reduces mostly the rapid eye movement (REM) stage of sleep [ZB: 311–327]. Whereas a little sleep loss does lead to drowsiness, tradeoffs soon occur. The added stresses also initiate compensatory mechanisms. These lead to greater arousal responses and tend to heighten one's attentiveness [ZB: 510–513, 584–588; ZBR: 185–187, 237–239; SI: 127–128]. As meditators increase their capacities for concentration, they begin to notice that they feel *less* tired, even though they are spending fewer hours sleeping in bed at night.[6] Most retreats close on an invigorating upbeat note, leaving the positive impression that one's mature capacities have expanded in the course of the whole experience.

Recent research clarifies how the human brain sleeps and reacts to different kinds of sleep deprivation.

Background: Sleep Studies in Normals and Meditators

Certain person's circadian clocks are programmed to enable them to sleep longer than others. Long sleepers (those whose sleep lasts more than nine hours) also show a delay in their morning adrenal cortisol peaks. Their cortisol peaks occur two to four hours later than do the peaks of short sleepers (whose sleep lasts less than six hours).[7]

When Ioannides and colleagues studied normal sleep, their high-resolution MEG techniques identified a large "core" region (five cubic centimeters) in the *left* dorsomedial prefrontal cortex.[8] Gamma activities increase in this core region during REM sleep to levels even higher than when we are actively awake. These extra-high prefrontal gamma activities during REM become of further interest with regard to the possibility that some aspect of a tonic REM phase might present a setting potentially receptive to a triggering stimulus. The tonic REM phase has been linked with the brain's general tendencies toward a greater degree of "residual alertness" and auditory reactivity [ZB: 316–327].

Gujar and colleagues studied how losing sleep affects the brain's functional MRI activity during the later resting state.[9] Their group of sleep-deprived subjects stayed awake throughout day 1, night 1, and day 2. This meant that they had spent an average of 35 hours in prolonged wakefulness. The subjects lost substantial amounts of *both* slow-wave and REM sleep. This loss clearly interfered with their ability to remain vigilant during goal-directed performance tasks. In contrast, the *non*-sleep-deprived control group maintained conventional degrees of attention-induced deactivation within their midline anterior and posterior brain regions.

Ong and colleagues prescribed a course of mindfulness meditation plus cognitive behavioral therapy for twenty-one patients whose chief complaint was insomnia.[10] When the patients were surveyed 6 and 12 months later, those who had greater mindfulness skills had also shown significant improvements over their prior daytime sleepiness. On the other hand, their night-time insomnia had not necessarily improved.

We await a comprehensive, longitudinal, multidisciplinary comparative study of the way particular meditative training programs influence individual meditator's sleep patterns and the way meditators perform during the daytime [ZBR: 141–146].

Part V

Daily Life Practice

Familiarity with the workings of the emotional household is the first step in the training.

Myokyo-ni (1921–2007) (Irmgard Schloegl)

14

Preconditions for Fruitful Practice

Zen is everywhere. But for you, Zen is right here.
Master Shunryu Suzuki (1905–1971)[1]

Zen is right *here* in your daily life. Right *now*, in your emotional household. The past is gone, the future is not here yet. Just this present moment is real. Just this. Each new day of meditating more selflessly in the everyday world brings fresh opportunities to explore optional ways to transform your unwholesome thoughts, opinions, speech, and actions.

- **Align yourself with the basic age-old guidelines governing wholesome intentions and ethical conduct.**
  The basic principle of restraint (Sanskrit: *shila*) is straightforward: an ounce of prevention is worth more than a pound of cure. Today's restraints and renunciations anticipate Self-centered, unfruitful behavior patterns and toxic situations, enabling you to steer a more skillful, practical course in the future.

In his sermons, the Buddha tailored his message to fit each audience's practical needs and levels of understanding. On one occasion,[2] he specified which *preconditions* served to create a propitious setting for wisdom to develop along the eightfold noble Path [ZB: 355–358]. Presented here in a simpler conventional format, these factors are:

- *Find a teacher whom you respect*, **to whom you can turn for sound advice.**
- *Live within the dharma, exercising virtuous restraint and rectitude in body and mind.*

- *Learn, remember, and integrate the traditional teachings into your daily life practice.*
- *Follow wholesome habits and live energetically.*
- *Practice mindful introspection* to discover why you cling to certain thoughts, feelings, beliefs, and perceptions, and can't let go of them.
- *Join a sangha,* a community of like-minded seekers.[3]
- *Play an affirmative role in your sangha.* Avoid trivial talk and gossip.

* * *

But what if I'm too set in my ways for such "New Age" practices, and too old to fit in with a group of mostly younger people?

The practices themselves are old-fashioned, and have been tested for two and a half millennia. Recent psychological studies by Nisbett and colleagues at the University of Michigan indicate that older mature adults have something to contribute: they show better reasoning abilities about how to resolve social conflicts than do their cohorts in younger age groups.[4] The fact that increasing age contributes to their development of wisdom was evident "at every level of social class, education, and I.Q. level." Men and women did not differ in their aggregate wisdom. Nor were academic researchers any wiser than nonacademics who also held postgraduate degrees. Elsewhere it has been speculated that long-range meditative training could itself help nurture and accelerate some of the basic neurobiological processes of maturation that enter into general problem solving, emotional regulation, and personality development [ZBR: 394–401; SI: 237–244].

Background: Age-Old Zen, Poetry, and Calligraphy

The liberal arts make subtle contributions to the whole cultural setting in which intuition can be cultivated and wisdom slowly emerge in a human brain. In Japan, there's an old saying, "Poetry and Zen are one" (*Shizen ichimi*). Poetry practice is an integral part of Zen, both indoors and outdoors.

- **Reawaken your appreciation of the simple, direct, deep expressions of poetry.**
  In the clarity that follows meditating, you'll become able to read between the lines of subtle poetry with greater understanding. Moreover, selected samples of old Chinese and Japanese poetry can also help the reader comprehend which phenomena are unveiled during the states of insight-wisdom [ZBR: 432–438; 440–447].

In China, an old saying is "Calligraphy is a painting of the heart-mind" [ZB: 669]. When decades of brushwork by a Zen-trained calligrapher are analyzed by an expert's eye, they often reveal distinctive patterns of increasing refinement.[5] Not until Master Hakuin reached 79 years did his calligraphic writing truly reveal his inner self. That of the Buddhist nun Otagaki Rengetso occurred during her final year, at age 84. The true ability of Master Yamamoto Gempo was discerned when he was 80 and that of Master Kato Kozan when he was 94.

- **Stick with the practice. It wont be easy. Yet, as your anxieties drop away and you become more selfless, your behavior will keep evolving.**

15

Remaining Attentive Throughout the Day; Living Zen Practice

> Pay attention and quiet your mind as soon as you get up in the morning.
>
> Ch'an Master Yuan-wu (1063–1135)

> Direct your mind exclusively to what you are doing.
>
> Maimonides (1138–1204)[1]

> Meditation in the midst of action is infinitely superior to meditation in stillness.
>
> Master Hakuin Ekaku (1689–1769)[2]
> His final calligraphy

> Fortunately, (psycho)analysis is not the only way to resolve inner conflicts. Life itself still remains a very effective therapist.
>
> Karen Horney (1885–1952)

- **Life is a great teacher. Slow down. Pay undistracted attention to what's happening.**
- **Experience the way life unfolds on its own. You'll realize increasingly what a gift it is to share in simply being alive.**

  Meditative practices cultivate this appreciation through the fine art of precise, objective observation. Gradually, as the practices hone your attentiveness, you become aware of whatever happens right NOW in the world, internally and externally.

  Before long, of course, you'll find yourself ruminating about some trivial earlier irritation or your plans for the future. Sooner or later, involuntary, re-mindful awareness will realize that you had just drifted away from being mindful of each wondrous, mundane, present moment.

Re-mindful levels of awareness continue to reassert themselves in every setting throughout the whole day. Omori Sogen referred to such an ongoing daily practice as "Zazen without sitting."[3] As Master Hakuin also emphasized with customary vigor when he was younger, "To plumb the very depths of your true nature and to access that genuine power which enables you to act freely in any circumstance, nothing surpasses the practice of Zen in a state of activity."[4]

- **Pause. Focus the sharp point of attention on discrete events throughout each day.**
  Let go of the slightest Self-conscious intention that *you* "should" be doing it.[5] Let it happen. Instead of your usual, mindless habit of bolting down meals, eat more slowly. Pause. Allow time for your taste buds and sense of smell to savor each small mouthful.

Living Zen also involves pausing for mindful introspection. Pausing allows you to discover—*in your daily round of seemingly ordinary activities—what* you long for, and *what* you loathe. This entails coming to a clear-eyed, hard-nosed diagnosis. Precisely *what* is it that just turned you on, or off? In this pause, the next step is to analyze: *why* am I so opinionated?

- **Mindful introspection keeps serving as an antidote for your ignorance.**
  Similarly, generosity acts as a remedy for your greed, and simple acts of kindness gradually erode hatred [ZBR: 240–242.]

Living Zen practice cultivates humility. Everyday experiences teach you that you're still biased, ignorant, deluded about crucial interpersonal issues, and capable of being led way off course. Nor can you manipulate every circumstance just to suit your own obsessive needs for perfection [ZB: 76–77]. With time, you'll discover which situations are tractable and let go of your attachments to the others.

- **When problems arise in a relationship, try to discern why the other person has a different point of view. After all, this is what "other-referential" actually involves.**
  However, in any of life's partnerships, *you* are the person ultimately responsible for resolving your *own* internal feelings of discomfort.

- **Let little cues refresh your short-term and long-term attentive memory functions.**
  When you're driving and stop for a red light, consider using it as a simple reminder to *look up*. This red light can become an excellent way to channel impulses through the fusiform gyrus and the other-referential networks down along the lower occipital → temporal pathway (figure 4). *Really* focus attention on *just this* percept—this red area off at a distance—while you're waiting patiently for the light to change. No other concepts or associations are part of this practice.[6]

- **Be courteous to other drivers when you take the wheel.**
  Don't feel that you're losing some inalienable "right." Let other drivers go first for a change. Yield, without needing to have any yellow sign that instructs you to yield. Cultivate similar degrees of patience with other persons throughout the day.

- **Be generous in donating your seemingly personal belongings to other persons.**
  Generosity is the first among the six virtues to be perfected by a bodhisattva.[7] Much of what you think is "yours" has actually been donated in the form of generous gifts from the rest of the world. Keep passing it on. Develop the habit of giving valuable things away. You can't take them with you. Be stingy only in your intrusive need to share your many liabilities with others.

16

Learning "Good" Habits Through Repetition: The Fruits of Meditative Practices

Habits are sequential, repetitive, motor or cognitive behaviors elicited by external or internal triggers that, once released, can go to completion without constant conscious oversight.

A. Graybiel[1]

The great end of life is not knowledge but action.

Thomas H. Huxley (1825–1895)

We were born with instincts for survival. On these, we superimposed acquired, automatic patterns of habitual thought and behavior. These habits perform themselves. We aren't always in there, "doing" them. From long experience we've learned that good habits are hard to establish; bad habits are very hard to extinguish [ZB: 189–196, 327–336, 653–659; ZBR: 248–250, 396–398]. Instincts seem impermeable to our best efforts.

Actions speak louder than words. Only constant repetition enables the fruits of meditative practice to arrive. It's helpful to *in*habit these actual *experiences*. They help us to learn. Getting further "inside," and actually attending to trial-and-error experiences, we learn which new tactics, strategies, and overall policies are worthwhile. When we learn motor routines through habitual practice, we engage in what psychologists call a *procedural* kind of learning. Learning to ride a bicycle is one such procedure. We don't confuse the highly tangible kinesthetic aspects of bike riding with those abstract kinds of higher cognitive learning that enable us to encode simple facts and discrete events into complex, intangible thoughts. The latter are examples of so-called *declarative* learning. (We can "declare" this factual information to other people.)

Patients who suffer from disorders of their basal ganglia (see later discussion) have problems learning new procedures. For example, they can't learn how to find their way through a maze. Instead of responding automatically, they need to focus constantly on particular sensorimotor associations. In contrast, patients who have medial temporal lobe lesions around their hippocampus can't recount (declare) facts, nor can they retrieve from memory episodes that they had recently experienced.[2]

The first phase of learning is very goal-oriented and Self-conscious. This is true whether we are trying to ride a bicycle or learning how to meditate on a cushion. We must pay explicit top-down attention as soon as we take either seat. Much later, bicycle riding and meditating become increasingly reflexive and involuntary. Finally, they tend to "happen." During these later stages, our top-down levels of consciousness are no longer explicitly aware that the brain is automatically performing an enormous number of implicit, subconscious computations. "Out of sight," stays "out of mind."

This chapter opens the lid of this former "black box," and peers down inside to examine the origins of our habitual behaviors. We'll then consider how cultivating certain meditative practices might help transform some negative habits in more fruitful adaptive directions.

Background: The Role of Circuits that Loop Between Basal Ganglia and Cortex

The thalamus provides a crucial model for understanding meditative training (chapter 12). Recent research also points toward further interactions that involve the basal ganglia, an extended cluster of deep nuclear structures. Many early steps in our procedural learning involve the nucleus accumbens down in the *ventral* striatum [SI: 205–206]. Prominent slightly later in behavioral functions are additional circuits at the next higher level. These next two nuclei, up in our *dorsal* striatum, are the caudate nucleus and the putamen. Pathways rising from the midbrain release dopamine in both of these levels of the striatum [ZBR: 251–255]. Dopamine contributes to the energies that drive our underlying motivations. It also helps us assign values to the different contingencies that can help guide our next course of action.

Byzantine interactions exist among any looping circuits that link the basal ganglia and thalamus with our cortex. They determine which sensorimotor representations will be "chunked" into elementary sequences. When these networks aggregate into larger programs, they start to express our habitual patterns of thought and behavior.[3] In the simpler systems of the mouse brain, direct measurements implicate the dorsal *medial* part of the striatum earlier in learning, aided by glutamate neurotransmission.[4] In humans, this association region would be roughly analogous to the dorsal part of our caudate nucleus. In contrast, the dorsal *lateral* part of the mouse striatum is engaged during the later sensorimotor phases of learning a skill. This region is rough-ly analogous to the human putamen.

The term *implicit* is usefully applied to the particular learning skills that we develop *non*intentionally. These skills continue to evolve without our being consciously aware of them. Many implicit learning skills are referable to the densities of dopamine D2 receptors in the ventral ("limbic") part of our striatum.[5] Here, the nucleus accumbens is the site of major interconnections with our amygdala and orbito-frontal cortex. Other recent studies suggest that the human brain leans an activist bias only toward behaviors that reap the most imminent of the rewards that are available. This inclination to act *now* is represented among the networks that link our ventral striatum with the self-other continuum in the medial prefrontal cortex and posterior cingulate regions.[6]

An apocryphal story describes the hungry donkey who was deficient in "horse sense." Why did he starve to death when hay was so readily available? Because his front feet were planted equidistant from the bale of hay off to either side and he couldn't make up his mind. Fleming and col-leagues created a human version resembling this situation, "when in doubt, do nothing."[7] In brief, their recent behav-ioral and fMRI study implicates a nucleus lying under the thalamus. This *subthalamic nucleus* plays a pivotal role both when we engage in an outright suppression of responses *and* when the slowing or switching process is more con-trolled. During such a vitally important role, which higher region sends this subthalamic nucleus its crucial top-down messages? The *right* inferior frontal cortex.

Suppose human subjects receive an unexpected sensory cue. It abruptly shifts their visual attention. Now another distinct network is also activated. Its loops link parts of the basal ganglia with the anterior cingulate gyrus and with the dorso-lateral-fronto-insular regions.[8] Which parts of the basal ganglia are involved? They include the dorsal medial part of the globus pallidus and nearby regions of the caudate nucleus and ventral striatum. The intriguing functions of this independent network also resemble those of a circuit used for "cognitive control." Its components could prove useful when we need to activate new attentional sets and/or to inhibit competing processes.

Can meditation really influence my habits in so many ways?

When you first sit down to meditate on the cushion, you've already begun a subtle, multilevel, unconscious approach to character change. Can these changing patterns of impulse flow translate into a change in your learned behavior? Yes, under one condition:

- **You can actualize what you learn about yourself on the cushion only when you repeatedly practice it in your daily experiences in the outdoors, at home, at work, and in the marketplace.**

No words in this book are to be interpreted as suggesting that neural Buddhism is some abstract esoteric or academic topic. Instead, the intention is to point you toward a Living Zen. Living Zen is grounded in repeating fruitful behavioral practices and in directly experiencing the fresh living reality of the present moment [ZB: 76–77; SI: 13, 203].

Sure, one learns new behaviors best by direct experience, not through concepts. But how does this difference translate into the actual learning processes that occur down at the level of individual nerve cells?

Let's say that one is simply drying off one's face in a towel as part of a morning ritual. In this act, looping circuits engage the sensorimotor cortex with the basal ganglia, thalamus, and related subcortical structures [ZB: 399–402]. This chapter emphasizes the key roles that the upper and lower levels of the striatum play in these loops.

The striatum also shares an intimate relationship with important neurochemical messengers other than dopamine. These molecules comprise the glutamate → nitric oxide → cyclic guanosine monophosphate (GMP) system [ZBR: 279–288; SI: 260–261]. This system's intriguing properties already suggest other plausible mechanisms that can help us learn good habits. As yet, their sequences are untested in humans. Animal research suggests that these are basic neurochemical mechanisms that enable the repeated normal fluxes of our major excitatory transmitters—glutamate and acetylcholine—to set in motion other crucial secondary effects. And these, because they begin with a covert release of nitric oxide, could then go on to subtly modify our motor patterns of behavior and reshape many habitual cognitive functions.

A long-term, balanced program of meditative training offers opportunities for nitric oxide to exert its potentially transforming effects at multiple levels, both acutely and chronically. For example, it is plausible to consider that future research might reveal the ways that nitric oxide-induced transformations could sculpture the steps through which some earlier phases of our procedural learning in the ventral striatum and caudate nucleus shift later to involve sequences in the nearby putamen. Noteworthy in this regard are the structural MRI studies reported in experienced Zen meditators.[9] Pagnoni and Cekic found that regular repeated Zen meditative training practices correlate, not only with the preservation of sustained attentive skills, but also with the sparing of the meditator's left putamen from the age-related shrinkage found in matched controls [SI: 243–244].

Commentary: Repeated daily life practices (*shugyo*) become the agency of incremental brain change. To practice Living Zen is not easy. It is to make repeated selfless, skillful, adaptive, behavioral concessions to everyone else with whom you interact in an ongoing relationship.

This means developing inherent capacities to subordinate your pride and its own precious "needs." It involves considering the *other legitimate interests and needs* of family, friends, roommates, team members, partners, spouses, babies, children, teenagers, teachers, fellow employees, and employers, etc. In all such negotiations, you learn slowly, through trial and error, which are the optimum times, places, and ways to assert *or* submerge your previously overconditioned Self.

Myokyo-ni defined all this as "Acceptance Practice." It was "an attitude of service, of consideration for what is . . . a slow practice of ripening, of becoming whole."[10] Decades of these practical, real-life experiences slowly sandpaper off and erode away the hard-edged habitual behaviors layered around the flagpole that raised the banner of your old, sovereign Self. Living Zen bows, palms together, and accepts this lower profile.

In short, are you suggesting that one's attitudes and habitual behaviors will actually begin to embody the ways that the brain is gradually becoming more other-referential?

Yes. [ZB: 668–677]. Suppose you were then to ask: What are some ideal fruits of such a long-term meditative practice? A short answer would include a humane being whose increasing capacities for generosity and compassionate behavior now extend skillfully outward not only to humanity and the environment at large but also inward to nourish the no less legitimate interests of that smaller-sized, lower-case self back in the center.

On the Everyday Practice of Gratitude

Gratitude bestows reverence, allowing us to encounter every-day epiphanies, those transcendent moments of awe that change forever how we experience life and the world.

John Milton (1608–1674)

When eating bamboo sprouts, remember who planted them.

Old Chinese Proverb

Buddhism grew new roots when it was transplanted into Chinese soil. There, the earth was already well sown with indigenous Taoism and Confucianism. This new Ch'an school of Buddhism would emerge in a form that was more earthy, practical, less cerebral. Gratitude seems also to emerge in a similar manner, as though its taproot were grounded in an elemental creative process. Had something almost umbilical developed back in those formative months when we were mere inches long, blind as Milton, enveloped in darkness, totally dependent on maternal warmth and nourishment?

We were amazingly lucky to have emerged and devel-oped in the form of a sentient human being. Our different cultures keep expressing their thanks in various forms of social behavior. Native Americans practiced indigenous customs for giving thanks long before the Pilgrims cele-brated "our" Thanksgiving in 1621. Judeo-Christian cultural traditions commonly include mealtime graces with thanks for life's many blessings. East Asia, in particular, has been observing ancestor-worship ceremonies for millennia, cele-brating both the prior assistance of previous generations and the sense of their continual spiritual presence.

As a preamble to the contents of this chapter, a personal commentary is relevant. An early bout with severe pneumonia shaped my decision to be a doctor. My style of teaching always focused on helping others find the most prompt, effective therapy for their patients. True, I've said a silent prayer for some of my very sick patients in the past, certainly when members of my immediate family were ill. Yet there's never been the expectation that some higher power would intercede to aid my efforts and improve the patient's outcome.

Both at the laboratory bench and in clinical research, I soon discovered that I could never solve complex problems without the help of other persons. In candor, for the foregoing reasons, I feel most comfortable uttering words of gratitude for the *past*, for the countless ways that many other beings, whether still living or dead, had helped to shape real events that had actually happened. These were events that substantially changed my own life or the lives of other persons close to me. One of my limitations is that I tend not to be easily motivated by words and concepts that would project wishful thinking toward imaginary future scenarios, or that would express make-believe hopes for the general wellbeing, or future health and happiness, of humanity in the world at large.

A decade or so before I started Zen training, I started to compile a long list. It acknowledged the invaluable contributions that many generations of persons, and a few animals, had made throughout my personal and professional life.[1] Then, around 1983 (two years after kensho), the formal practice of gratitude arose spontaneously. It would soon become the prelude to each morning's meditation (chapter 6). By then it seemed to have entered my life almost as involuntarily as breathing. This morning practice of gratitude expanded over the years. It went on to include almost every human being (and three memorable dogs) with whom I have ever had significant contact.

Doesn't their contact with you imply that this is entirely a Self-centered frame of reference?

Looking in from the outside, you might at first think so. Yet from the inside, it *feels* different. It feels more like the expansion outward of some instinctual behavior, coupled with an overview that celebrates an entire *Self-other continuum*. In this all-inclusive sense, gratitude practice becomes an open celebration of others that never seems centered exclusively in my Self. I've tried to express such a difference in visual terms elsewhere.[2]

Gratitude practice evolved, especially following retreats, to include saying a silent grace before breakfast, to giving thanks after a trip to all drivers and pilots whose skillful efforts brought the traveler safely back home, and to an occasional expression of thanks before dropping off to sleep at night for some significant event during the day. The practice now seems simply an appropriate way to behave, a quiet ritual unattached to notions of primary or secondary personal gain.

In later decades I've been introduced to some *metta* (loving kindness) practices of Theravada Buddhism. These made it increasingly possible to include a deepening sense of gratitude for other major challenging events. Seemingly negative at first, these were prompted by other people's actions. However, when other people irritated me, they also exposed my own prejudices, ignorance, and unskillful behaviors. Applying conscious effort, I've learned to rechannel constructively the energies that come from the resulting internal conflict of ideas.[3] True, it is difficult to maintain such degrees of objective, unattached understanding. It is much easier to welcome life's full range of harmonies—not its dissonances—as the gifts of simply being alive.

- **Repeat little acts of actual kindness until kindness becomes a habit.**
  Go beyond merely thinking kind thoughts.

- **Remember that life has a lighter side, full of humor, comedy, and a welcome release in laughter.**
  The comic perspective has a well-developed historic role in Zen [ZB: 413–418; ZBR: 165–167]. Perhaps you need further reminders of the fact that when you were born you were automatically cast in a minor role in life's comedy of errors. If so, you might consider perusing the latest collection of humorous quotations just published by Oxford University Press.[4] Or, if you're a visual person, you can find memorable cartoons about dogs[5] and doctors[6] in the old *New Yorker* collections. Some of these might also happen to strike your "funny bone."

Finally, although some notion of "happiness" enters only tangentially into gratitude practice, it does so in a manner rather different from the way many contemporary cultures define what it means to be happy.[7] One common misunderstanding is that happiness always means success, that you'll be happy only when you can keep on extracting *more* of what you want from life or from other people, be it material goods or interpersonal satisfactions. I've come to realize that genuine happiness arises in simply being grateful for whatever actually exists, in *just this present moment*, and for the innumerable blessings inherited from the past.

Background: Gratitude

The Buddha discerned that the egocentric perspective was our basic major liability. What was the ultimate happiness? Being liberated from one's prior concepts of Self. Thus his words in the sutra saying, "Getting free of the conceit that 'I am'—this is truly the greatest happiness of all."[8]

In the Satipatthana Sutra,[9] the Buddha suggests that other mental qualities also arise *naturally* along the Path of meditative training. In fact, these relate directly to the re-mindful emergence of gratitude. One of these evolving attributes consists in "honoring the benefits one has received." The other development inclines one to reflect on the inspiring qualities of the larger spiritual tradition one has inherited. It applies in particular to the inspiration one had received from certain teachers. Kobori-Roshi learned from his own teacher where Zen meditation would lead. As a matter of course, it would be to this natural spontaneous feeling of gratitude, one that would be shared with other persons. Indeed, his teacher added, "without gratitude, meditation is not enough."[10]

Research in recent decades has linked this impulse to "count one's blessings" with a greater sense of well-being and optimism in general.[11] In a recent study of 221 young adolescents, the practice of counting one's blessings was associated with the positive attributes of optimism, life satisfaction, and with a decrease in negative affect.[12] Remembering how rapidly adolescent attitudes change, it is significant that the students who were the most grateful were also those who remained most satisfied with their school experience at the time they were followed up three weeks later.

Studies suggest that adults who are more religious also tend to have higher levels of emotional well-being.[13] These correlations are interpreted as expressing an implicit mode that is "self-regulatory." In this instance, the self-regulatory restraint on behavior is *not* viewed as an intrusion that has been consciously Self-imposed from the top down. Instead, it is regarded as an implicit, Self-correcting positive attitude that remains "flexible, efficient, and largely unconscious." We seem to be in the presence of another long-term, overview attribute, a silent presence of mind. It can operate skillfully in the present without needing to be consciously prompted.

A moderate degree of pervasive cheerfulness is one personality trait associated with emotional well-being. This falls short of becoming "Pollyannaish." The State-Trait-Cheerfulness-Inventory provides a reasonably reliable way to assess such a buoyancy that still enables some persons to respond cheerfully—chin up, as it were—in spite of life's many negative events.[14] In a recent pilot study, ten male subjects completed this questionnaire. Those who gave evidence of a general predilection toward greater cheerfulness later showed more fMRI activation in their right inferior parietal lobule when their task was to view various humorous versions of Gary Larson cartoons. The authors point out that this is a different finding from the way that the limbic regions of the brain respond more when subjects first understand a joke and then develop an emotional reaction to the joke [SI: 136–141]. If a larger, high-resolution study of this trait were applied longitudinally to meditators, it might provide interesting data.

18

Opening Up into Silent, Preconscious Processing

> There is a guidance for each of us, and by lowly listening we shall hear the right word.
> Ralph Waldo Emerson (1803–1882)[1]

Everyday life presents different sized problems. Ideally, we address them with a seamless blend of procedural skills led by our top-down and bottom-up forms of attentiveness. Living Zen cultivates this natural, flexible, balanced, best-of-both-worlds approach. Over the decades, an increasingly clear consciousness begins to see through the many veils infused with unbidden impressions that had previously obscured our vision. Hindsight and foresight let us begin to appreciate our implicit inclusion within the environment "out there" as *IT* really is, right now.

Unfortunately, a hectic twenty-first-century culture keeps us missing this "big picture." Daily, we're entangled not only with words that are spoken and printed on paper, but now with blizzards of words generated on electronic screens. Overwhelmed in such a world, it's too easy to fall back on the assumption that the way to solve all complex problems is to use words that we can hear ourselves think, *consciously*. (After all, if we *think* these word-thoughts, most must really be true. And if we also *say* them, they really are true).

Reviewed elsewhere are decades of evidence that suggests otherwise [ZB: 358–386; SI: 153–173, 183–188].[2] Indeed, our brain often proceeds surprisingly well, thank you, as soon as we start to let go of our high-minded linguistic approach and get out of our own intrusive way. Then, in solitude, what do we rediscover? Our lower pathways of "lowly listening." These wordless insights are our guidance systems. They are innate, tacit, intelligent, Self-correcting systems. Using covert modes of processing, their codes confer "right" choices *intuitively, silently*. Sotto voce hunches tap levels of implicit comprehension. These have yet to coalesce into words that we can hear ourselves think.[3]

- **Explore diverse practices that, by minimizing the intrusive Self, allow your highly competent automatic pilot to operate intuitively, insightfully.**

Is this why the Zen approach to meditative training tends to favor a style of "no-thought," silent, global, attentive processing?

The paths leading toward insight-wisdom seem to have been discovered centuries before Zen arrived. The fact that intuitive capacities emerge from lowly silent listening probably began as a soft, empirical observation in many lands and spiritual disciplines. Generations since appear to have rediscovered these paths empirically [ZB: 633–636]. When Emerson spoke of being guided by such "lowly listening," he began by saying that in our everyday efforts it would prove fruitless to exercise only our [top-down] willpower alone. Why? Because that's not where our real strength comes from: "Only in our easy, simple, spontaneous action are we strong."

Background: Words that We Hear Ourselves Think, as Distinguished from Silent Modes of Preconscious Processing

Table 3 elaborates on the basis for such distinctions. Their attributes are complementary. The table suggests a plausible rationale for a balanced program of meditation. It will be one in which the silent, global forms of spontaneous attentive processing could play an increasingly prominent role. The table blends earlier discussions of preattentive processing [ZB: 278–281; SI: 35–39] with a recent review of this important subject by Dijksterhuis and Nordgren.[4]

The table summarizes the two generic approaches we use when we try to solve difficult problems in daily life. It turns out that our problem-solving performance actually improves when we include covert intervals of intuitive preconscious processing. These complement the other intervals during which we can still employ to our advantage some assets of the styles of declarative conscious processing often accompanied by words that we hear ourself think.

Preconscious does not mean something exotic or mystical. Here, it simply refers to one's *potential* to include more intuitive mental processes. These subconscious mental processes can operate highly efficiently at times when no consciously heard thought sequences have infiltrated the mental foreground. The neurosciences have not yet adequately mapped the semantic terrain (let alone the neural traffic patterns) of such "seemingly no-person-in-there" kinds of deep

Table 3
Complementary Attributes of Conscious and Preconscious Problem Solving

Aspect	Conscious Thought Processing	Preconscious Processing
Operational definition	Top-down attention focuses on a task in the near-presence of conscious thoughts.	Bottom-up attention gravitates automatically toward subconscious processing in the absence of pertinent thoughts.
Egocentric or allocentric participation	Often overtly Self-referential.	Covertly other-referential.
Attached to word-thoughts of left hemispheric origin	Explicitly attached (lexical entanglement).	Free (implicitly non-verbal and ineffable).
How much effort is involved?	All "paying" of attention is effortful.	Insightful processing "realizes" effortlessly.
Speed	Slow serial processing in a small field.	Fast parallel processing of a large field.
Capacity	Low, 10–60 bits per second. Limited by the need for short-term working-memory storage.	Seemingly unlimited, perhaps ±10 million bits per second in the visual system.
Does it follow some underlying scheme or general system of analysis?	Yes, in a convergent manner, often confirming some kind of biased expectancy or cue.	Yes, but in a covert, divergent, and highly improvisational manner.
Initial impressions	Often more stereo-typed, polarized, fixed.	Often more creative, neutral, labile.
Later, is the person satisfied with earlier final decision?	Less so	More so
Are the results consistent?	Less so	More so

Table 3
(continued)

Aspect	Conscious Thought Processing	Preconscious Processing
Do more complex situations impair the accuracy of the final decision?	Yes, but accuracy improves if more time is devoted to voluntary problem solving.	Accuracy is impaired relatively less by complexity. Accuracy improves if the duration of active *incubation* (involuntary problem solving) is increased.
Can it follow strict rules, as in arithmetic?	Yes. It can accomplish fine degrees of critical analysis based on tight references.	No. Its "realizations" break established "rules." They provide more global, crude estimates based on loose references
Can it process negations easily (e.g., "not good")?	Yes, and it also discerns discrepancies more easily.	No, yet it also accommodates paradoxes more readily.

Source: Adapted from ZB: 24–25, 278–281 and from A. Dijksterhuis and L. Nordgren. A theory of unconscious thought. *Perspectives on Psychological Science* 2006; 1:95–109.

comprehension. However, it's abundantly clear that when no first-person Self intrudes into the procedures of preconscious processing, intuitive closures and insightful states can then take place with extraordinary speed, skill, and prescience.[5]

Meanwhile, as this whole field is still in the process of gathering data [SI: 153–173], the contrasts between the conscious and preconscious styles of processing already give rise to an important testable hypothesis. Let's state it simply, in the form of a question. When our *lower* temporo ↔ frontal pathways are less entangled in narrow wordy distractions, will they then become more wide open to engage in the free associations and creative play that give rise to the most adaptive insights? It is noteworthy that the brain assigns two major pathways to service a fast-track exchange between our frontal and temporal lobes. In front lies the uncinate fasciculus; behind is the superior longitudinal fasciculus.

Centuries of serious Zen training have remained compatible with paradox, blasphemy, and joyous laughter [ZB: 414–415]. Zen's subtle aspects continue to spring surprises on its unwary trainees, many more than they could possibly imagine at first. A most distinctive aspect of Zen is the way it employs a riddle to entice and baffle the logical, ever-questioning mind. Can the trainees solve this riddle by using their most prized cognitive asset—their conscious, declarative thought processes alone?

With this question, we turn in the next chapter to consider koan practice at much deeper levels. Here, incubation, re-mindfulness, and lowly listening can be guided by preconscious processing.

19

Koan Practice at Deep Levels

> The koan is not given as an object to understand. It is given to you to solve your own problem . . . to manifest yourself as a perfect being.
>
> Joshu Sasaki-Roshi (1907–)

A koan is an artificial concentration device, a metaphor that points toward great unanswered questions[1] [ZBR: 61–64, 273]. You can't "solve" a koan using your discursive intellect. It can be resolved during a state of insight. The shift into this intuitive mode represents a radical psychophysiological departure from the ordinary train of conscious, logical, thoughts you are using to read this page or to solve other problems.

You are not usually assigned a koan until you can bring to calm, mindful introspection a substantial degree of attentive competence and objectivity. Subsequently, the fact that you keep incubating your koan, or its short summary (capping) phrase, helps you retrieve it usefully as soon as you're reminded that your mind is now preoccupied with some wandering thought, image, or feeling.[2]

What good does it do then to spontaneously recall the short capping phrase that condenses your koan?

It can help begin to exercise some longer-term, automatic, remindful functions involved in *sati* (chapter 11). Trainees can simply recall this summary phrase, using it to suspend both their mind-wandering and their usual tendency to overintellectualize the whole question. Cleary interprets such a superficial usage of the koan as "an immediate alert system using a very direct Zen technique" that can help trainees clear their mental vision.[3] As he then explains, cultivating one's inherent capacity "to bring enhanced attention to bear on any object at will gradually develops into a spontaneous ability to direct attention autonomously." Of course, this is more likely to occur only to the degree that receptive meditative techniques are *also* practiced, the kinds that encourage involuntary bottom-up attentive processing to develop spontaneously.

However, koan practice can lead far beyond this preliminary monitoring of attention on so limited a field [ZB: 107–119, 540–542]. From this point on, it's easy to concede that we still know relatively little about the millisecond neural sequences of introspection, incubation, and remindfulness in general (chapters 11 and 12) [SI: 153–158]. And yet, somehow, it seems that incubating a koan's oblique resonances of obscure meaning does help *indirectly* to nudge one's intuitive processes. In which direction? Toward more expansive associations, some of which might rarely coalesce later inside states of direct comprehension. Belatedly, these rare events could enter one's open field of consciousness in the form of insights that convey the impression of "universal principles and objective reality." The column at the right side of table 2 in the previous chapter cites simpler aspects of these other-referential, insightful, preconscious kinds of processing. On the rare occasions when a genuine, deep, psychic vacancy of Self occurs, their association networks seem to open up—effortlessly, silently—into the realization of "all things as *THEY really are.*"

Long before such a happening, the first koan often given to beginners poses this question: "Does a dog have Buddha-nature?" Old Master Chou-chu's response was "No" (*wu* in Chinese, *mu* in Japanese) [ZBR: 61–64]. Why might it even have been helpful—when you first encountered this un-expected "No"—if you were a person who loved dogs and overvalued logic? Because you would have two good rea-sons for immediately rejecting the premise of this koan. You would then be thrown straight back into an immediate expe-rience: your own Self-righteous feelings of indignation and disbelief. Your rejection of the "No" answer would serve to highlight why *direct experience* has long been emphasized in Zen. To actually feel such opinions grinding away inside helps you realize that these are *your* emotions at work.

The same two-letter word "No" has other valuable uses during Zen. As Kobori-Roshi explained, it is the direct way the Zen master "gradually conditions away years upon years of his students' unfruitful thinking and behavior" [ZB: 61]. Beyond this, many old koans still sound so nonsensical that they pose a severe test of one's abilities to tolerate ambi-guities. Can you learn to accept a "not-knowing" situation? Can you incubate your own ignorance for a very long time?

- **Be patient with a koan.**
  Incubation proceeds at a glacial pace. It can take years before little intuitions draw tighter the net of asso-ciations that might help resolve its deeper layers of allusive meaning [SI: 153–188]. Meanwhile,

*Don't blame a koan for leaving you perplexed. That's what it's supposed to do.
The koan serves as a barrier to the endless branching of every wordy, intellectual thought and undercurrents of emotion.

In fact, it's an asset to be suddenly baffled and to remain baffled, to *not* know. To endure such a condition of *not-knowing* helps keep you more alert, more open to any and all possibilities. Teachers learn (having once been students themselves) how valuable it is to pose rhetorical questions. Recent studies hint that our ignorance can become a virtue *if* the challenge motivates us to keep searching whenever we don't know the answer.[4]

A koan doesn't seek mere factual information. The thirty fourth koan in Master Wumen's collection of forty-eight koans even includes this explicit comment by Master Man-ch'uan (748–835): "Knowledge is not the Way." He goes on to explain that when the subtle act (of intuition) realizes truth, this is a state not only free from passion but also beyond "the realms of perception or cognition."[5] A major psychic and physical sense of release (Sanskrit: *moksha*) occurs when there is a deep resolution of issues alluded to in the koan. It relieves the trainee of the burdens imposed by other indirect issues that are of the trainee's own making, including the sense of remaining frustrated by not-knowing [ZBR: 234].

Background: Koan Practice at Silent, Preconscious Levels

At the beginning, a koan might seem to be a "juicy intellectual worm," useful to bait the hook and guide potential trainees toward a more serious level of practice.[6] On the other hand, because a koan often points *indirectly* toward the enlightened mind state of some ancient worthies who lived in a much different cultural era, do you really need to wrestle with it intellectually, as though it were a contemporary twenty-first century narrative? You will wrestle, whether you need to or not.

The koan is a paradoxical statement. It is important to appreciate that when kensho's brief state of deep insightful consciousness resolves the koan, it will also cut the neural root of *all* paradoxes. This is a resolution *at the core of paradox itself*, not simply an intellectual reconciliation of the koan per se. This state of insight-wisdom also resolves all the other clashing dualities created by our own prior overconditioned concepts.[7] In fact, it was understood back in ancient China that at the very moment "when these koans are understood and accepted, then there will be an end to feeling and discrimination."[8] This brief oversimplification of life's previous emotional polarities can remain impressive, at least for the next several days.

During the more advanced practices of introspecting a Zen koan, both trainee and teacher enter into an intimate dyadic relationship. The subtle dynamics of their interactions seem likely both to encourage, and to promote, various degrees of what is increasingly recognized as *implicit learning*. Why is implicit learning per se not obvious either to the insiders or to the casual onlooker? Because it develops during *subconscious* attentive processing (table 3). As Dijksterhuis and Aarts explain, implicit learning enables people to learn "complex rules and relations between events that they encounter in a bottom-up fashion without being aware of them."[9]

Skeptical readers might object. Aren't these two authors playing a shell game, like the psychoanalysts who've alleged that events take place, hidden out of our sight, down in some mysterious unproven depths of the "unconscious"? Judge for yourself whether the authors had conducted a biased review of subconscious processing.[10] Can a reader appreciate how crucial is the role that *covert* attention plays in their formulations? Yes, it's hinted early, by the fact that Dijksterhuis and Aarts start by *clearly linking attention with processing*. Indeed, when defining attention, they even propose this elegantly simply wording: attention is "the extent to which incoming information is processed."

Subsequently the two authors then proceed to review the substantial evidence showing that *subliminal* goals (of which we remain largely unaware) do influence our *bottom-up* attentive processing. Notice that even though we might previously have made such goal-driven decisions *subconsciously*, a casual onlooker might later be misled by our subsequent "good" behavior, thinking that it must have been the result of voluntary, well-planned, conscious decisions. Instead, the weight of the evidence indicates that the real origins of such (implicit) behavior were determined at *involuntary* subconscious levels (chapter 16).

This recent research on implicit, preconscious learning has an intriguing sidelight. Even though the trained subjects do improve their problem-solving performance, they're *often still unaware that they have, in fact, been learning anything*. Why? In Freud's metaphor, all of our usual conscious knowing is merely the tip of an iceberg. This superficial component of our mental operations can little appreciate the huge bulk of ice that lurks underneath it.

A future comprehensive, longitudinal study of the many mechanisms of neuroplasticity in meditators could not only contribute much to our understanding of insight in general and selfless insight in particular. It could also help clarify how subconscious attentive processing continues its silent, affirmative guiding role among the hidden re-mindful levels of our psyche.

20

A Quickening Evoked by Re-mindful Hearing

Barn's burnt down.
Now I can see the moon.

Kusunoki Masashige (1294–1336)[1]

I'm still not clear: How can regular meditation practices that train attention enable my brain to change in ways that might lead to enlightened states?

Repeated periods of meditation sensitize our receptivities and enhance some reactivities selectively (figure 7) [ZB: 198, 454, 457–460; SI: 82]. A regular program of meditative training cultivates pauses that uncover, and glimpse, operations at subconscious levels we've not been aware of. "Opening up" meditation enables more of these little openings to occur.

Earlier chapters emphasized the pathways that process visual stimuli. However, one's hearing pathways also become more sensitive. Early in my own practice I noticed how certain auditory stimuli evoked a reactive response. Sound stimuli became especially penetrating after only two or three days of repeated quiet sittings during retreats. Then, each "crack" of the mallet on the large wooden board outside the meditation hall caused my ears to "click."

This is nothing special; you can experience the same click in your own ear. Simply swallow. You *hear and feel* the click. It's your middle ear muscles tightening your eardrum. It is reasonable to postulate that this click reflects a local brainstem reflex, a sensorimotor arc that becomes enhanced when repeated periods of meditation sensitize a person's dopamine, norepinephrine, and a variety of other neuromessenger circuits [ZB: 197–208]. In this manner can regular meditation practices develop a variety of "mind-manifesting" properties [ZB: 418–426].

The following narrative serves to illustrate the dynamic range of such emergent, receptive properties. It describes only a minor quickening [ZB: 371–404]. Yet the results were relayed up instantly from the brainstem into higher reactive networks. These instantly retrieved information from years ago that had lain dormant in my brain's subconscious recesses. The message is that subconscious traces of earlier coded events remain in our long-term memory banks for more years than one can imagine.

Case Report: A Recent Auditory Quickening

It is January 2008. I am sitting in the zendo at Upaya during a retreat. Multiple sittings have taken place during the previous two days and two sittings have already taken place this morning. I am turning to the right and looking slightly up to hear Roshi Joan Halifax. She is speaking 15 feet away. I'm hearing her say three words: "Barn's burnt down"— the first three words of the epigraph that introduced this chapter.

Audition is on a hair trigger. Instantly, a major, prickly cold wave of "gooseflesh" begins over the back of my head and neck. It runs down the back of my arms and trunk, then down the back of my *right* leg more so than my left. The closing line registers a distant sense of recognition: "Now I can see the moon." During the next second or so, a flood of tears issues from both eyes. It continues much more abundantly down my right cheek than the left for the next half minute.

This quickening includes a much greater pilomotor (gooseflesh) response than I have ever experienced before.[2] It is obviously more lateralized (to the right), and it has released much more tearing (also right-sided). Curiously, no corresponding wave of emotion accompanies the bare twinge of recognition. For centuries, Zen students have been prompted to ask their temporo → frontal lower pathways:

What is this? The neurologist also wonders: *What* has been going on?

Background I: Coda

For many summers barns were a significant ingredient in the author's boyhood experiences.[3] Yet this particular haiku didn't enter into my consciousness until the year 2000. The first time I encountered these two spare lines was on an ordinary 3 × 5-inch file card. Someone had appreciated their message, copied it, and posted this card on the bulletin board outside the zendo of our Mountain Lamp Sangha in Moscow, Idaho. The words resonated, so I copied them down on a file card of my own. It promptly disappeared for the next eight years.

It is tragic to lose one's barn in a fire. Thereafter, deprived of possessions, one could feel impoverished and hard-pressed to survive. Instead, we discover this poet who is undaunted, buoyant. Why? Now, he can see the moon rise. It fills the empty space where his own barn once stood and obscured the sky above the horizon. Liberated by his loss, he is free to bathe in the serenity of moonlight [ZB: 577–578].

The poem unfolds one hidden symbol after another. (In much the same way, we slowly realize the many depths of meaning involved in Zen Buddhism.) What flames had consumed that barn? Could its burning hint at the same fires that Buddha referred to in an early sermon? He suggested that the heat of our emotions was what caused us to suffer. Our longings, loathings, and delusions of Selfhood were responsible.

And what was the structural support in the roof of the barn that had collapsed? It was the lofty ridgepole of Self-deception that had gone down in ashes. No more could its

spine support the rafters serving as a ribcage for an emotionally overconditioned Self [ZBR: 6].

What does it mean to "see the moon"? It means that only after every Self-centered obstruction vanishes from view can one's brain realize the stark, cool clarity of objective vision. During such an awakened state of consciousness enlightenment simply means *seeing all things as they really are*. In such allusive ways does the old Zen literature connect the moon's ineffable light with an extraordinary state of selfless mental illumination [ZBR: 403–463].

To this meditator, *barn* was no four-letter word that could be heard lightly, no word forever misplaced on some file card. It resonated with me because seven decades earlier, barns fragrant with cows, horses, and new-mown hay were an intimate part of my everyday summer experience. "Barn" was imbedded deeply in my lived experience. Barns and I shared a *déjà vécu* history, as it were. This vignette illustrates one more instance in which repeated periods of meditation, acting as a catalyst, have set the stage for a brief, re-mindful quickening.

Surging into experience, quickenings tap into networks looping high and low. They connect the links of symbolic and autobiographical memory traces that could have lain dormant for decades. In the previous chapters on preconscious processing and koans, it was suggested that authentic, advanced koan practice might have a subtle, hidden role to play in a program of balanced meditative training. Here, we're not referring to some obvious top-down intellectual role. Rather might such a role lie in its dynamic potential to help open up deep layers of *implicit* meanings and values. These might be widely dispersed in the form of coded hints and associations not accessible to a person's ordinary rules of conscious, logical processing.

The reactions to the poem that morning also have implications with regard to some of the *unsentimental*, emotionally *unattached* qualities that develop later along the meditative Path. Similar qualities of objectivity also infuse kensho. For example, on this occasion, despite the florid autonomic phenomena of gooseflesh and tearing, the psyche of this meditating witness developed *no* corresponding tug of an emotional feeling. This uneven profile of diverse phenomena suggests that the several components of an episode of quickening can be fractionated. Perhaps in an older person who had been meditating for decades, the neural trajectory of the activations does not always ascend through the limbic system to mobilize higher levels of emotion [SI: 228–244]. Parenthetically, the selfless realizations and insights that arrive during the state of kensho enter free from the immediate attachments that could bind them to the very different, culturally acquired, intellectual propositions of religious ideology.[4]

Background II: Hearing Pathways in Relation to Quickening

Normally our hearing pathways conduct: (1) the ultrafast, "hot-line" auditory messages that race up through the inferior colliculi and pulvinar; and (2) the usual fast messages that rise up through the medial geniculate nucleus of the thalamus [ZB: 240–244]. The colliculi are for immediate reactions. They service our lower, hot-line, reflexive pathways. The geniculate pathway relays from the thalamus up into the cortical networks which service our higher degrees of conscious cognition.

On the other hand, certain kinds of relevant sensory stimuli are quickly shunted into messages that relay into our hypothalamus. From here they descend in the autonomic nervous system, soon emerging on the skin's surface as the phenomenon we call "gooseflesh." These pilomotor pathways began their surge into activity just as I was hearing the next five words of the second line.

What about the ascending hearing pathways, the ones that could also enable impulses coded for words like "Barn's burnt down" to rise up through the pulvinar and geniculate nuclei of the thalamus? These messages—now tagged with salient properties—speed up toward the region of the *right* temporo-parietal junction that includes the *right* superior temporal gyrus [SI: 32, 133–134, 140]. This right TPJ has been assigned a priority function (figure 2). It serves as our "circuit breaker." This phrase describes the way it enables attention to *disengage* from its previous orientation, so that it can shift instead toward the newly salient stimulus.

From then on, implicit auditory messages can be decoded by the pattern-recognition functions distributed along the temporal lobe networks that engage in bottom-up attentive processing. A relevant finding is the way that Lutz and colleagues have shown how expert meditators, long practiced in a Self-induced form of loving-kindness-compassion meditation, respond to sounds with a greater activation of their right TPJ and their right posterior superior temporal region.[5]

We're not the only animal species sensitive to certain sounds. Tears flow from the eyes of a distressed mother camel when she hears plaintive music. These musical sound vibrations trigger a pivotal shift of her mental set. The result softens her emotional distress, liberates her native maternal instincts, and allows her to nurse her previously abandoned newborn colt [SI: 146–149].

Positron emission tomography (PET) scans were used in an early study of human subjects who were undergoing an intensely pleasant emotional response to music. During their so-called shivers-down-the-spine phenomena, blood flow actually *decreased* in the right amygdala, left hippocampus, and ventro-medial prefrontal cortex.[6] One explanation for the author's emotional *unattachment* during the auditory quickening in the zendo might be a similar decrease in activity of the particular circuits of the right amygdala that convey positive emotion. The pilomotor "chills" described in this personal vignette were also lateralized more to the right. This suggests that the *un*crossed pathway descending from the *right* hypothalamus was the more sensitive on this occasion, as was the parasympathetic tearing response from the right eye [ZB: 189–196].

Henke's recent review of short-term and long-term memory systems emphasizes the fast, implicit processing mechanisms that instantly engage our hippocampus and parahippocampus, not just the distinctions based simply on whether or not we then become conscious of this information.[7]

The immediate reactivity during this episode of quickening illustrates the speed with which the brain accomplishes so much. Some reactive circuits seemed to complete their initial closures in milliseconds, long before the concluding word of the poem was uttered. To begin to study such early sequences will require the millisecond resolutions of the latest magnetoencephalography spatial techniques. Already, the three- to six-*second* lag of the usual fMRI signals seems too sluggish.

Behavioral tasks were recently assigned to experienced Vipassana meditators who were *not* meditating during the study.[8] The subjects reacted less during this complex intersensory (visual + auditory) facilitation task. The data were interpreted as suggesting an attenuation of their lower level, bottom-up attentive processing. In normals, fMRI signals in the ventral attention system are suppressed during those more deliberate searches which also require the subjects to focus their top-down attention.[9]

Having encouraged readers to pay bottom-up auditory attention afield, let us close with a selection from the notebook of the poet, Rainer Rilke (1875–1926). His pen still

speaks to how a penetrating avian stimulus could set off a concordant unification over a century ago.[10]

"... a bird-call was there, both in the outside and in his inner being" ... a call that did not stop at the boundary of his body. Instead, it "formed of the two together an uninterrupted space." Herein, "mysteriously protected, only one single spot of purest, deepest consciousness remained."

21

A Ripened Fruit of Practice: Cut Wide Open

> All is empty, clear,
> revealed effortlessly, naturally.
> Neither thinking nor imagination
> can ever reach this state.
>
> Master Seng-ts'an (died 606)[1]

Suppose you had devoted not just a few months, but years to cultivating a balanced, mindful, introspective meditative practice [ZB: 125–129]. This in itself would be unusual; most beginners drop out or practice half-heartedly. But then suppose something else happens. After many years on the slowly ripening Path of practice, an unexpected grace note of selfless insight-wisdom suddenly arrives. In Zen, such a rare state of deep, clear, cool realization is called "*kensho*" or "*satori.*" Many have tried to explain what this "sound of a great Amen" feels like. However, words can't convey the penetrating quality of prajna's lightninglike flash of insight [ZB: 542–584; ZBR: 333–371]. Nor do words exist that could accurately translate the neural codes of such a so-called peak experience.

Having identified his psychological attachments to the notions of a Self as the root cause of his own suffering, how did the Buddha refer to this abrupt release from such bondage? The analogy served to bring the experience down to earth. No, it wasn't the arrival of some high-minded, lofty intellectual concept. Instead, it was the way a lowly butcher operates when his sharp knife is wielded skillfully. This razor-sharp cut cleanly severs every tendon and ligament that previously held the joints of a skeleton together.[2] Not with bells, whistles, and fanfare from on high, but in this surgical manner does prajna's sword-thrust of insight-wisdom instantly disarticulate every delight, lust, inner defilement, and clinging that had been the deeply rooted cause of our basic angst.

A butcher's knife? This was a striking image. Consider the Hindu cultural setting and the historical era in which it appeared. Does disarticulation convey an accurate impression? Could this be how one actually experiences such an extraordinary state of consciousness [ZBR: 5–6; SI: 201–202]? Yes. Kobori-Roshi had also employed the evocative phrase, "a cut in the mind," when he described such an incisive moment to me. Using body language, how did he present his answer to the above questions? He demonstrated how deep this valley was by fully extending his two arms and hands way down, with fingers touching, into a long V-shaped gesture [ZB: 109, 654–659].

The ancient patriarchs also understood from their own direct experience that so deep a release from the bondage of our conditioning (Sanskrit: *moksha*) could not be the result of the keenest logic or leap of imagination. Indeed, in the Judeo-Christian tradition, such a total release would be described as that "peace which passeth all understanding." And the early Christian meditative traditions gave the term *kenosis* to the deep emptying process that could liberate each personal Self from its overdriven fears and passionate attachments.

The ancients also understood that that most valleys are eroding gradually, that "awakening" occurs at a seemingly glacial pace, not only suddenly. When the word *insight* occurs in the context of meditation in the Tibetan tradition, it often tends to refer to a particular kind of *additional* investigation, one that is slow, ongoing, probing, and thorough. Such an analysis provides, *incrementally*, a succession of useful smaller insights. These too can gradually break down the cortex of a long bone into its fragments, expose the marrow, and begin to extract the underlying nature of reality. First, however, the meditator must develop a substantial degree of stable inner tranquility and objectivity. Only then can this analytical procedure be sufficiently accurate to operate effectively over the range of practical Self/other issues. In most meditative traditions, such a keen, ongoing, fine-grained, discerning analytical faculty remains an essential component in the contemplative meditator's quest for deeper existential wisdom.[3]

- **Merely sitting passively on a cushion per se does not suffice.**
  Remember: "No-thinking" refers to letting go of our unfruitful, emotionally driven discursive ruminations. Meditative calming allows the energies driving these thoughts to drop away. In the resulting silence and solitude we're left with more open, undistracted time, space, and mental clarity. In this quiet setting, implicit modes can also incubate issues slowly, remindfully, at subconscious levels that we're not aware of. More conscious forms of analysis finally begin to discern the root cause of each dissatisfaction and start realizing which remedy to apply to it. These several Self-correcting steps can evolve with clinical

detachment during the so-called silent illumination kinds of meditation (chapter 10). Mindful introspection is useful to the degree that it becomes more objective and increasingly selfless. However, no Self glides smoothly toward any subordinate role. Expect turbulence along the way.

You've now been proposing a long list of different suggestions for meditators. What about constructive advice for researchers in general?

In brief, the message might condense into these four "Ds":

- **Devise ingenious nonintrusive signaling methods in order to access the actual details of each subject's mental landscape during meditation.**
  We need accurate, semiquantitative, moment-by-moment measurements of the actual ongoing qualities of this evolving mental landscape in skilled, well-trained meditating subjects. Preliminary studies starting with well-trained subjects suggest the applicability of approaches based on multivariate pattern analysis.[4]

- **Deploy more target stimuli in the peripheral visual and auditory fields.**
  We need better ways to measure the more peripheral, bottom-up skills that develop in the course of reflexive attentive processing.

- **Develop accurate, meaningful terminologies.**
  We need a much more accurate semantic understanding of events that take place within this whole new field. Consider two examples. The first concerns the earlier phrase, "task-positive regions." Task-positive pointed more toward what the early *researchers'* task might *add* to the experiment. Yet, even a phrase like "attention-*on*" regions might serve as a more accurate

and meaningful description. Why? Because it could help specify the fact that attention modules actually turn "on" when the *subject's* brain first reacts to every task. When does a "cognitive load" begin? When attention starts to *"turn on"* out at its pointed tip (Figure 1). Continuing this line of reasoning, even an unusual phrase-like "attention-*off*" regions might serve as an optional description of the reciprocal sequences involved. Often such a phrase might be more accurate than such now-usual phrases as "task-negative," or "default" regions.

The second example concerns "monitoring." This word fits easily into an accurate description of our ordinary, top-down, short-term, working-memory forms of surveillance. In a sense, they keep track of successive individual trees. Yet, "monitoring" seems out of place if its use is relegated *solely* to the category of our long-term overview, *re*-mindful functions. These operate more covertly and intuitively during the kinds of evolved forms of receptive meditation that open up a globally receptive landscape to include whole forests of larger issues.

- **Define which functions of the deeper brainstem-thalamic-basal ganglia circuits enter into the mechanisms that mediate the inverse relationships between our attentiveness and Self-centeredness up at the cortical level.**
  Fundamental bioelectric, metabolic, and neurochemical mechanisms are lurking—unidentified—among these reactivities and slow intrinsic fluctuations. We must understand these mechanisms in order to clarify how the different wave forms detected using EEG, MEG, and fMRI methods can be correlated with each meditating subject's conscious experience at *that precise* moment.[5]

In Summary: A Sequence of Topics to Help Clarify the Mechanisms of Selfless Insight-Wisdom

> Stop splashing along the surface with all your words and concepts . . . dive down deep into zazen.
>
> Nanrei Kobori-Roshi [ZB: 108]

> In order to discover who you are, first learn who everybody else is. You're what's left.
>
> (Inside the author's fortune cookie, May 2010)

To meet meditators' practical needs, most explanations in the previous chapters have already been oversimplified. As we begin to summarize them here, it helps to return to a basic question: Why does Zen emphasize the training of *attention* during our actual daily life practice?

Millennia before "Zen" became a word, the early teachings identified three crucial Self-inflicted troublemakers. They were our emotional fires—our longings for, our loathings against—and our delusions of Self. Their flames consumed us with dissatisfactions. Successive generations then discovered something interesting: The more they practiced the techniques that trained attention, the more their Self-centered fires of greed, hatred, and ignorance tended to die out. Behavioral psychologists in the past century would suggest that such greedy longings lured us into "approach behaviors," and that our loathings generated "avoidance behaviors." Nowadays, even fortune cookie sayings can rephrase ancient words of insight-wisdom, providing nourishment for the psyche in unexpected ways.

We're fortunate to live in an era of neuroimaging research, although it is still at the dawn of its potential. Today, most researchers know that their attempts to correlate the structure of the brain with its interactive functions are still far from complete. Even so, it is already possible to glimpse a few basic organizing principles. Among them is the important evidence that our modules of attention relate *inversely* to some dynamic contours of our omnipresent Self (chapter 2).

Here, we now venture to condense, reconfigure, and share such a glimpse. To what end? To provide a tentative explanation for meditators, one that might encourage them to develop a more flexible, balanced, long-term program of training attention. Why? To enable their earlier Self to evolve. In which direction? Toward more mature forms of simplified, stable, adaptive behavior that can become increasingly selfless and compassionate. This is a tall order.

Can the general outline and dialogue on the next few pages present complete scientific proof for every suggestion made in this slender book? No. It can begin to assemble their components into a provisonal system of more logical sequences. These aren't always easy to follow, so read slowly.

The sequences described here begin as *pairs of opposites*. The resulting perspective unfolds in accord with the old Taoist point of view. Each yin and yang pairing that follows translates first into a set of elementary principles. Successive pairings then become stepping stones for understanding the concluding section of questions and answers. Aided by this dialogue, the resulting discussion clarifies how the earlier pairs of complementary opposites could become so reconciled that the different orchestral sections of our brain function in concert.

Most pages of any such musical score won't be composed until later in this century. Today, prudence dictates that our notations begin with simpler words and terms that point toward psychological concepts. They'll prove useful when trying to explain the relationships among such huge topics as attention, Self, and meditation.

Notice two of the key words: *voluntary* and *involuntary*. Voluntary implies that we've made a conscious, deliberate choice to perform a particular activity. Involuntary means that an action seems to *happen by itself*, spontaneously, reflexly. We've not explicitly chosen to make it happen. Indeed, we might be completely unaware that it even exists. Why? Because such an activity of thought or behavior often develops first at wordless, subconscious levels (or is buried there and retrievable only later).

The *preconscious processing* considered in table 3 of chapter 18 helps clarify why one goal of advanced meditative training is usually left unstated: to liberate our wordless, spontaneously creative, deeply affirmative *implicit* habits of mind and body. They happen to flow involuntarily, un-Self-consciously. Six previous chapters have presented a neural-Zen perspective on these subtle, preconscious, intuitive operations (chapters 15–20). This orientation toward implicit learning represents a direction that I believe Zen has been coming from for many past centuries. Clearly, the evidence at present still seems softer than that obtained using today's standard academic approach to behavioral neurology.

The outline begins with:

1. **Our two basic *cortical systems of attention*. They are**

    Top-down (figure 1) and bottom-up (figure 7)

    Dorsal and ventral

    Upper and lower

    More voluntary and intentional, more involuntary and unintentional.

2. **Our two basic versions of *processing ordinary reality*. They are**

    Self-centered (figure 3) and other-centered (figure 5)

Egocentric (**E**) and allocentric (**A**)

Self-relational and other-relational (figure 4)

More voluntary, more involuntary

3. **Our personal Self expresses the underlying operational functions of a kind of "I-Me-Mine" complex:**

   We refer its tangible aspects to our physical body—our somatic Self, our soma.

   Its intangible aspects are referable to our mental states—our psychic Self, our psyche.

4. **Evolution sculptured our brain to meet urgent needs: personal and group survival. Sometimes now, just to survive, we still resort to those deep, instinctual programs. But what do we usually need most urgently? Not more emotional reactivity per se. No. We need *to let go of* old rigid, over-conditioned emotional biases in order to respond creatively to each new challenging circumstance. The following pairing provides an example of such opposite attitudes:**

   Dispensible: Our sovereign, rigidly biased, *I-Me-Mine* Self.

   Indispensible: The subordinate, flexible, intuitive, i-me-mine self.

5. **With respect to the different (but complementary) ways to train our brains and bodies, the two basic categories of meditation are**

   Concentrative and receptive

   More voluntary and focused, more involuntary and open

There are five sets of conceptual pairs here. They began with words that relate to three general topics: attention, Self, and meditation. Why do we now need to explain how each of these sets relates to the others? Because the deep lingering question remains: How can a brain simultaneously delete all its personal, *Self*-centered frames of reference, yet still unveil its covert resources of *other*-referential attentive processing? This means that we must next translate attention/Self/ meditation in terms that refer to functional anatomical sequences. (Although the full details of these topics and sequences lie far beyond our present scope, readers who have a special interest in psychophysiology will find their correlates recently reviewed elsewhere [ZBR, 2006; SI, 2009].)

So now we continue the outline aided by words that translate the five earlier conceptual pairs in terms of their physiological and anatomical origins:

6. **With regard to *physiological* functions, our two basic *modes* are**

    Excitation and inhibition

    Activation and deactivation

7. **Researchers use PET scans and functional MRI scans to reveal which particular brain regions are normally undergoing these two contrasting functional events. The resulting brain images use warmer colors (red) to indicate greater activity and cooler colors (blue) to represent lesser degrees of activity. On brain "maps," their respective color gradations resemble hot spots and cool spots.**

8. **The top-down and bottom-up forms of attention each generate their hot spots of activity in two very different regions (figures 2 and 4).**

    Top-down attention generates its hot spots on each side, *symmetrically*. These active modules localize chiefly in the upper regions of each parietal lobe (IPS) and frontal lobe (FEF). In contrast, bottom-up attention generates chiefly *right*-sided hot spots. They arise lower down, in the *right* temporo-parietal junction and in the *right* inferior frontal cortex.

9. **We have two major pathways that process "reality." Each one frames reality from its own unique perspective.**

The egocentric pathway dominates. It processes reality in a *Self-centered* manner (**E**). Its upper trajectory pursues an upward course through our dorsal occipito → parieto → frontal regions. Along this upper route, its 3-D coordinates refer their lines of sight back to the axial center of our *somatic* Self (figure 3). Why back to our physical Self?

A crucial point: This is because much of the information flowing along this "northern" (dorsal) Self-centered trajectory overlaps two important nearby regions. The first overlapping includes the two IPS and FEF sites of our *dorsal*, top-down attention systems. The second overlap includes our sensory *association* cortex. It is located up in the superior parietal lobule. This upper parietal region is *responsible for articulating the separate parts of our body into a schema representing our somatic, physical Self.* The result is that regions all along this upper trajectory become uniquely qualified. Their task is to ask and answer the practical egocentric question: *Where* is this apple *in relation to Me* (figure 4)?

In contrast, the subordinate pathway pursues a much *lower*, occipito → temporo → frontal trajectory (figure 4). Its frame of reference occurs independently, involuntarily, and in an other-referential (allocentric) (**A**) manner. From this allocentric perspective, *no* lines of sight point back to the body *or* the psyche of any observer in the center. It asks: *What* is this?

Note that the *ventral*, bottom-up system of attention resides a relatively short distance away from this "southern" processing trajectory. Therefore, when an external stimulus captures the attention of the bottom-up system, this lower (**A**) pathway can be accessed relatively easily.

What does this functional anatomy mean for meditators?
It has three important implications:

1. Suppose you follow Kobori-Roshi's good advice. You learn to "dive deep into zazen," gradually letting go of words and concepts. At such deeper levels of meditation, you will be accessing resources that refine your more *involuntary* forms of bottom-up attention. The more you learn how to really *let go*, the more will the resulting processing evolve at implicit, subconscious levels. This will happen on its own. Your Self-consciousness will not be informed that tacit processing is involved.

Notice that these bottom-up practices of attention are referable more to the *right*-sided cortical networks in the lower regions of the brain (figure 2). The habitual cultivation of bottom-up attentive practices could gradually enable you to access more readily the multiple interpretive functions nearby within your lower temporo ↔ frontal pathways. Their more intuitive contributions could then be included among those that normally enter into your everyday allocentric processing.

2. These lower networks on the *right* side enable your attentive processing to represent *both* sides of the outside world. They also help you respond to the total global environment in a more reflexive, other-referential manner.

3. The third aspect of the lower temporo → frontal networks is also referable to this *right* side: they are not burdened by the same heavy commitment to language as are their counterpart regions over in the *left* hemisphere. Ideally, by not talking during retreats, by not hearing other persons talk, and by not reading, the resulting silence could tend to free more circuits on both sides of your brain from being entangled in language. The calming aspects of meditation also serve to minimize the otherwise strong tendency

for discursive word-thoughts to rise up and contaminate your mental field. By reducing the general "noise" level of language processing, these internal and external measures enable each incoming auditory signal to stand out above the background. Thereafter, when a random triggering signal enters, it can have a more effective impact.

I'm understanding this concept of the physical Self, my body schema, my soma. Its harder to understand how much of my Self— my "psyche"—might be represented.

The evidence suggests that the intangible Self of our psyche is widely distributed. It is represented among higher interactive functions that are cognitive, emotional, and subtly autobiographical in nature. But two of the largest regions referable to our psychic Self are located deep inside the brain (chapter 5). These medial regions lie along the *inner* frontal and parietal surfaces of its right and left hemispheres (figure 6).

Several lines of evidence converge to suggest that a basic, inverse seesaw relationship exists between these representations of Self and external attention. What is the basis for such a reciprocal relationship? One plausible working hypothesis would begin with a deep midline structure—the thalamus. All nuclei in the *dorsal* tier of this thalamus normally engage in oscillatory interactions with their partners up in the cortex. These thalamic nuclei help generate our Self-referential activities. Where? How? By stimulating the many cortical regions that represent the psychic Self *and* those dorsal regions that represent our somatic Self along the egocentric pathway (**E**) (as described in chapter 4 and figure 4). Notably, the three limbic nuclei up in the front of this dorsal thalamus are normally responsible for transmitting emotionally charged conditioned messages up to the cortex.

Fortunately, because the *reticular nucleus* covers the outside of the thalamus, it can act as a pivotal inhibitory "gate." This enables the brain to shift its balance—simultaneously—*away* from our old dominating somatic and psychic Self-centeredness and *toward* its other-referential modes of *selfless*, intuitive, allocentric, attentive processing.

So what's the bottom line of this nine-point outline and discussion in terms of meditating selflessly?

A living Zen perspective emerges from this neural Zen model. It views meditating selflessly as a very long term incremental process. When we carefully balance its two complementary practices of attentiveness, the blend serves to enhance not only the focusing and stability inherent in our attentional processing but also its flexibility *and* global scope.

Advanced meditative training practices cultivate the potentials of our innate Self-correcting capacities. Gradually, over decades, they enable deep set points to shift. As the fortune cookie message points out, the shift is *toward* more open, compassionate relationships with everyone else and *away* from that habitually in-turned, egocentric person we used to be. On rare occasions, during a major, so-called peak experience, such a shift from ego- into alloprocessing also happens acutely. Some neural residua of this brief episode can become deeply etched in long-term memory, helping to transform one's subsequent consciousness and to gentle one's behaviors [ZB: 653–659].

Highly complex issues are involved in meditative practices. These model proposals represent only first, tentative approximations. The narrative is ongoing.[1] Before this century closes, we should have a much clearer understanding of how brain and body interact normally, how they also respond affirmatively during a balanced program of very long-term meditative training, and how the actual details of a meditator's mental landscape correlate simultaneously with highly refined brain imaging techniques.

I can understand the last four sentences, yet all the earlier intervening steps seem too complicated to remember easily.

Hey, nobody ever said that a neural Zen perspective would be simple! Meanwhile, best wishes in cultivating re-mindfulness in your daily life practice!

Suggested "Do's" and "Don'ts"

These suggestions briefly summarize the main ideas proposed in the text. A program of meditative training includes many other techniques beyond the scope of these pages.

"Do's"

Preface

- Practicing doesn't mean you're obsessed with having to achieve perfection. Practice just means you're not perfect.

Part I An Introduction to Selfless Meditation

- Find some assurance in the evidence: meditation has been tested and found useful for millennia by many cultures and spiritual traditions.
- Follow Master Yuan-wu's advice: "Be even and balanced" in your attentiveness, becoming "attuned to the inherent equality of all things."
- Commit yourself to start simplifying your lifestyle. This is no token gesture toward letting go. It means that with disciplined restraint, you have finally decided to renounce particular longings and loathings identified as inappropriate. A more formal program of training can begin at this point.
- Note that you don't wall yourself off from experiencing life's vicissitudes. You still go on perceiving events in the real world.
  As Zen master Shunryu Suzuki said about impermanence, "Renunciation is not giving up the things of this world, but accepting that they go away."

- Your egocentric processing networks are hard-wired. They are already dominant. Be careful not to overuse them.

- You won't be Self-consciously aware of, or recognize, many "signposts" along the Path toward selfless meditation. Their subtle transformations will be evolving incrementally, at subterranean levels.

- Begin each meditation period by taking a slow, deep breath in; then slowly let it all flow out.
  This is a useful reminder: *Letting go is the essential operative mode.*

- Letting go means not striving for absolute perfection, yet still accomplishing the essentials.

- Lighten up.

- Inhabit bowing.
  Bowing remains an excellent way to begin one's formal practice before sitting down to meditate on a cushion.

- Allow bowing to genuinely express the fact that you are letting go of your own Self.
  Authentic bowing means that you are now—quite literally—lowering the flag of your sovereign *I*.

- Bow deeply from the waist as an expression of profound gratitude.
  Life—right *now, just this*—is an incredible gift.

- Extend your arms, wrists, fingers. Open up your gestures.

- Reorient attention, turning it outward.
  Choosing an external target relieves you of the obligation to pay so much effortful, focused, concentrated attention on separate regions of your whole physical body (your *soma*).

- Your regular meditation practices help refine a natural reflexive capacity. After it notices a lapse, it re-mindfully disengages, and instantly returns attention to its original focus. Repetition is the key word in the art of attending with competence to this subconscious domain. This capacity evolves very slowly.

- Notice thought intrusions. Then observe that they dissolve.
  Let agitated thoughts simply serve as a crude index of how much more you need to practice.

- Practice requires much patience, endurance, and discernment.
  You will need plain, hard-nosed courage to diagnose your own liabilities, sheer determination to persist in any endeavor that requires Self-discipline, and discernment to develop wholesome new priorities.

- Remember: It takes a long time to let go of your Self-imposed, top-down, endlessly cluttered emotional baggage.

- Be ready to test different meditative techniques yourself.

Part II Meditating Selflessly Outdoors

- Return often to the natural world. Take a walk by yourself for a change. Enjoy the solitude. Stay alert to its sounds, sights, and fragrances, to every feeling that its sensations evoke.

- Raise your sights. Expand your horizons. Allow your open-eyed gaze to involuntarily drift up into the distance.
  Out there, *involuntary awareness* has the potential to expand *far beyond the reach of your body*, into a whole wide world of natural scenery.

- Sharpen every listening skill. Listen in every direction.
- Listen to each of Nature's sounds.
- Remain alert to hear bird songs.
- Consider all the other delightful surprises of becoming a bird watcher.
  Gaze *up* to follow distant birds in flight. Bird sightings tap into our most primitive instincts and sentiments.
- Let your gaze drift up to witness the ridgelines of distant hills, up toward the peaks of any faroff mountains.
- Go out on a clear night, in solitude. Gaze up.
  Become aware of the moon, of the immense night sky, of its planets, stars, and constellations. Is one transient stardust Self on this small planet really so all-important?
- If you happen to awaken before dawn, go outdoors.
  Gaze *up*. In a clear eastern sky you'll often find the planet Venus at her brightest. Consider the implications of the legends about a man called Siddhartha who once *looked up*, and saw this same "morning star."
- A big old tree is one of Nature's gifts. Yield to any impulse to reach out and hug a tree.

Part III   Meditating Selflessly Indoors

- At first you settle "down and in."
  You begin as usual, by gazing *down* to focus on some discrete spot in front of you, say at an angle of around 45 degrees.

- Then allow yourself to experiment with different ways to follow your breath.

  Consider a simple "just this" approach.

- On some other occasion, as you settle down and in, begin to experiment by opening up the posture of your hands and arms.

  Discover the increasing degrees of freedom that can arise when you adopt a posture more open than usual. Openness applies to both your physical posture and to the attitude that pervades your mental posture.

- During the next stage you'll be experimenting with "turning up and out" almost everything about awareness that you had previously been turning down and in.

- Allow yourself to experiment with where and how you allow your gaze to rest.

  Cultivate practices that enable you to look up and out.

- Remember: Top-down attention is most efficient in focusing on targets down in front of you. This "conelike" convergence of visual attention is very different from the vast visual and hearing space that can open up to receive stimuli that arise from events far out there in the distance.

- Raise your eyelids when you feel drowsy and allow more light to stimulate your brain.

- Use tea or coffee judiciously.

- Be conscientious about your meditative practice, but follow the Buddha's more practical Middle Way, not the legendary excessive zeal associated with Bodhidharma.

- Notice how a totally inclusive presence of mind leaves no extra room around any of its edges for absent-minded lapses to occur.

- **Remain aware of whatever happens in just this present moment.**
  Begin by registering your percepts, thoughts, and emotions at the level of bare awareness.

- **Become a barometer, observing your own "inner weather," noticing how your arousal state, alertness, and emotions vary up and down.**

- **Accept with patience what might at first seem to be your limitations.**
  Remember that every mind wanders. Subtle *re-mindful* orientations operate *subconsciously*. It takes a very long time to further develop their trait skills.

- **If you would begin to walk the endless Path toward such enlightened traits, then it is absolutely essential to strengthen your practice by going on a retreat.**

Part IV   Attending Meditative Retreats

- **Sign up for a retreat. Show up and stay the course.**
  Keep reaching out toward the edge of your comfort zone. Expect parts of your psyche to put up stiff resistance. Examine all resistance.

- **Probe by asking: What is this resistance? Who is resisting? Why?**

- **Prepare a solid mental and physical foundation before you go on a retreat.**

- **Meditation, not medication.**
  Meditation is itself a mind-manifesting agency that leads to long-term character change.

- **Work vigorously between meditation periods.**
- **Pay close attention during walking meditation in order to become one with "Just Walking."**
- **Relearn the profound merits of solitude.**
  The practice of solitude is only a temporary withdrawal.
- **Maintain your practice of silence.**
  Extended silence takes on remarkable powers. It enables you to hear the still, small voice that otherwise languishes lowly within.
- **Avoid mirrors.**
  (Keep asking: *Who* needs to look?)

Part V   Daily Life Practice

- **Align yourself with the basic age-old guidelines governing wholesome intentions and ethical conduct.**
- **Find a teacher whom you respect**, to whom you can turn for advice.
- **Live within the dharma**, exercising virtuous restraint and rectitude in body and mind.
- **Learn, remember, and integrate the traditional teachings into your daily life practice**.
- **Follow wholesome habits and live energetically**.
- **Practice mindful introspection** to discover why you cling to certain thoughts, feelings, beliefs, and perceptions and can't let go of them.
- **Join a sangha**, a community of like-minded seekers.
- **Play an affirmative role in your sangha**. Avoid trivial talk and gossip.
- **Reawaken your appreciation of the simple, direct, deep expressions of poetry.**

- Stick with the practice. It wont be easy. Yet, as your anxieties drop away and you become more selfless, your behavior will keep evolving.

- Life is a great teacher. Slow down. Pay undistracted attention to what's happening.

- Experience the way life unfolds on its own. You'll realize increasingly what a gift it is to share in simply being alive.

- Pause. Focus the sharp point of attention on discrete events throughout each day.

  Let go of the slightest Self-conscious intention that *you* "should" be doing it. Let it happen. Eat more slowly. Pause. Savor each small mouthful.

- Mindful introspection keeps serving as an antidote for your ignorance.

  Similarly, generosity acts as a remedy for your greed, and simple acts of kindness gradually erode hatred.

- When problems arise in a relationship, try to discern why the other person has a different point of view. After all, this is what "other-referential" actually involves.

  However, in any of life's partnerships, *you* are the person ultimately responsible for resolving your *own* internal feelings of discomfort.

- Let little cues refresh your short-term and long-term attentive memory functions.

  When you're driving and stop for a red light, consider using it as a reminder to *look up*.

- Be courteous to other drivers when you take the wheel.

  Cultivate such patience with other persons throughout the day.

- **Be generous in donating your seemingly personal belongings to other persons.**
  Generosity is the first among the six virtues to be perfected by a bodhisattva.
- **You can actualize what you learn about yourself on the cushion only when you *repeatedly* practice it in your daily experiences in the outdoors, at home, at work, and in the marketplace.**
- **Repeat little acts of actual kindness until kindness becomes a habit.**
  Go beyond merely thinking kind thoughts.
- **Remember that life has a lighter side, full of humor, comedy, and a welcome release in laughter.**
- **Explore diverse practices that, because they minimize the Self, allow your highly competent automatic pilot to operate intuitively, insightfully.**
- **Be patient with a koan.**
  Incubation proceeds at a glacial pace. Years may pass before little intuitions draw tighter the net of associations that might help resolve its deeper layers of allusive meaning.
- **Merely sitting passively on a cushion per se does not suffice.**
  Mindful introspection is useful to the degree that it becomes more objective and increasingly selfless.

"The Don'ts"

*Don't expect to know precisely where you're heading, when you might happen to arrive, or what it means to be enlightened.
The "goalposts" keep moving farther on. . . .

*Don't expect to approach mature levels of balanced, selfless, meditative competence until you actually commit

yourself to meditating regularly and to practicing throughout the day.

Your lifelong, top-down, Self-centered habits, attitudes, and traits are too thoroughly rooted. This puts a premium on learning new ways to recognize your maladaptive Self and to let go of its dysfunctions. This enables its energies to be gradually transformed in the direction of compassion, skillfully deployed.

*Don't think that you should strive for artificially contrived movements. Rather, allow such behaviors to evolve involuntarily, unselfconsciously. They'll arrive as a natural by-product of long-term meditative training.

*Don't regard the concentrative and receptive categories of meditation as antithetical. However, if you allow your practice to overemphasize one category at the other's expense, such an imbalance could work at cross-purposes.

*Don't be discouraged when your thoughts tend to jump around like a restless monkey in a zoo.

Learn to be much more patient with your "monkey mind." In fact, it takes a very long time for one's turbid thought stream to slow down and become clear. In the interim, you will still be cultivating a gentle, *re*-mindful art; it *returns to the appropriate focus* whenever attention seems to stray.

*Don't think, Self-consciously, "I'm listening to that bird."

Instead, allow your ears to *hear its notes directly*. Just hearing.

*Don't cling to the notion that an episode of blissful absorption means you are enlightened.

*Don't think that you can become 100% "enlightened" by one brief awakening experience. Any first awakening serves merely as the beginning of the training.

During the next decades of your daily life practice, much further "sanding" will be needed to smooth off the multiple rough edges you developed earlier. And multiple sword thrusts that cut off the deep roots of Self are also necessary in order to realize every potential source of transformation.

*Don't blame a koan for leaving you perplexed. That's what it's supposed to do.

The koan stands as a barrier to the endless branching into this or that by every wordy, intellectual approach.

And as Constructive Suggestions for Researchers

- Devise ingenious nonintrusive methods in order to better assess the actual details of each subjects' mental landscape during meditation.

- Deploy more target stimuli in the peripheral visual and auditory fields.

- Develop accurate, meaningful terminologies.
  We need a much more accurate semantic understanding of events that take place within this whole new field.

- Define which functions of the deeper brainstem-thalamic-basal ganglia circuits enter into the mechanisms that mediate the inverse relationships between our attentiveness and Self-centeredness up at the cortical level.

A Sampler of Recommended Reading

This Century

Shodo Harada-Roshi. *The Path to Bodhidharma. The Teachings of Shodo Harada-Roshi.* (Ed. J. Lago) (Tr. T. Storandt). Boston. Tuttle, 2000.

T. Maezumi and B. Glassman. *On Zen Practice. Body, Breath, and Mind.* Boston. Wisdom, 2000.

Sheng-yen and D. Stevenson. *Hoofprint of the Ox. Principles of the Chan Buddhist Path as Taught by a Modern Chinese Master.* New York. Oxford University Press, 2001.

S. Addis, S. Lombardo, and J. Roitman (Eds.). *Zen Source Book. Traditional Documents from China, Korea, and Japan.* Indianapolis, IN. Hackett, 2008.

Old Favorites

S. Suzuki. *Zen Mind, Beginner's Mind.* New York. Weatherhill, 1975.

I. Schloegl. *The Zen Way.* London. Sheldon, 1977.

R. Aitken. *Encouraging Words. Zen Buddhist Teachings for Western Students.* New York. Pantheon, 1993.

J. Kabat-Zinn. *Wherever You Go, There You Are. Mindfulness Meditation in Everyday Life.* New York. Hyperion, 1994.

Some Secondary Effects on the Brain of Stress and Pathological Lesions

> . . . until you experience this: To die, and thus to grow, you'll remain only a troubled guest on this dark earth.
>
> Johann von Goethe (1749–1832)[1]

> It is only shallow waters that make a noisy, restless stream, while a deep whirlpool goes on silently.
>
> Master Soyen Shaku (1859–1919)[2]

As a neurologist, I'm often asked two kinds of questions:

What about the reports that certain strenuous meditative practices can "drive" a human brain into various forms of spiritual/ mystical experiences?

Conservative meditative traditions do introduce carefully cali brated stress responses. However, they tend to shun claims that spectacular paranormal mental powers might result [ZB: 235–240]. For example, Soyen Shaku was the first Rinzai Zen master to visit the United States, over a hundred years ago.[3] He specifically excluded various mental epiphenomena that can occur when meditation is conducted under excessively pressured conditions [ZB: 373–376].[4]

What about recent reports that gross brain damage to some cortical regions can also be linked with changes in Self/other perceptions, mystical experiences, and/or "spiritual" attitudes?

This book considers certain "subtractions" of physiological functions. Its suggestions are based on evidence in a category different from the dysfunctions caused by gross brain damage. However, an early relevant report came from Degos and colleagues in

1997.[5] In their patients, left-sided infarctions had caused substantial posterior cortical damage at the parieto-temporo-occipital junction [ZBR: 15–19]. These patients showed an apparent breakdown of the former boundary that stood as a barrier between their Self and the other world outside. The result was an overinclusive Self-centered frame of reference. One patient described the resulting impression as "everything was inside me." Various kinds of cortical dysfunction around the temporo-parietal junction were subsequently reported to cause other patients to further displace their center of Self-awareness during "out-of-body experiences" [ZBR: 211–214; SI: 264].

In 2006, Uddin and colleagues suggested that the region around the right TPJ and the adjacent inferior parietal lobule played a substantial role in Self/other judgments.[6] They based this on their use of transcranial magnetic stimulation (TMS) to create a brief disruption of the normal functions of the right inferior parietal lobule [SI: 196].

In 2008, Jill Taylor described a personal journey which began with the acute rupture of blood from a left-sided angiomatous malformation into a region "near the middle to posterior portion" of her cerebral cortex [SI: 152]. "By the end of that morning, my consciousness shifted into a perception that I was at *one* with the universe."[7] The nature and sources of the several qualities that can be associated with the word "Oneness" were reviewed elsewhere [ZBR: 333–357].

A recent neurosurgical series from Italy by Urgesi and colleagues[8] focused on the preoperative and postoperative personal reports made by their eighty-eight patients. All had brain tumors. These tumors were either malignant gliomas (68) or meningiomas (20). They were surgically removed from anterior (fronto-temporal) or posterior (occipito-temporo-parietal) brain regions. The patients' responses to a series of questions were taken to indicate their degree of "spirituality." Spirituality was indexed by testing a dimension of the personality called "self-transcendence."

At the time that the single *pre*operative interview was conducted, more patients in the group with gross posterior tumors already considered themselves to be "religious." They also rated higher in their "self-transcendence" test scores than did the patients who had anterior lesions, both before and after surgery. Surgical resections of gliomas that had invaded the right angular gyrus region and the left inferior parietal lobe were correlated with an "extended self-referential awareness." In contrast, meningioma removals (often a less traumatic procedure) were not associated with increases in "self-transcendence."

A critical discussion of how gross cortical brain lesions, white matter disconnections, corticosteroid treatment, edema, and operative brain damage can interfere with the way normal patients perceive the complex boundary between their Self and their environment is far beyond the scope of a book on meditation [SI: 152]. Suffice it to mention here three practical points:

1. The pathological nature of the reports cited would not lead the present author (let alone a hard-nosed Zen master) to conclude that acute gross cortical brain damage accurately reproduces *all* of the major psychophysiological manifestations of a kensho-like state.[9]

2. This book emphasizes a balance of the *physiological* mechanisms that can be cultivated by trainees who diligently pursue a program of long-term concentrative and receptive meditative practices. Most of these physiological mechanisms will be operating in the early milliseconds, not up in our cortex, but down among countless networks that interact at *sub*cortical levels.

3. As we continue to search for all of the mechanisms and sequences that enable meditation to transform consciousness, it would seem that more of such silent functions, operating down in Soyen Shaku's deep "whirlpool" of our subconscious, would merit increasingly re-mindful attention and careful investigation.

References and Notes

For the reader's convenience, the text uses brackets [ ] as a way to cross-reference topics that are discussed further on the pages of the three earlier books in this series. Thus *Zen and the Brain* is abbreviated [ZB:__], *Zen-Brain Reflections* is [ZBR:__], and *Selfless Insight* is [SI:__].

Preface

1. T. Cleary. *Classics of Buddhism and Zen*, vol. 2. Boston. Shambhala, 2001, 5.
2. J. Austin. *Selfless Insight. Zen and the Meditative Transformations of Consciousness*. Cambridge, MA. MIT Press, 2009, 269.
3. D. Brooks. The Neural Buddhist. www:nytimes.com/2008/05/13/opinion/13brooks.html?_r=. Brooks mentions that one of the relatively novel ideas to emerge from neuroscientific research into meditative states of consciousness is the belief that "the self is not a fixed entity but a dynamic process of relationships."

By Way of a Personal Introduction

1. J. Austin. *Zen and the Brain. Toward an Understanding of Meditation and Consciousness*. Cambridge, MA. MIT Press, 1998. Hereafter often abbreviated as [ZB]. The term *Roshi* is used as an honorific for a respected Zen master. The word is said to have arisen from the way Japanese lips and tongue transposed r and l when they pronounced the name of Lao-tzu. In Chinese, these words mean "old master" and they also referred to the name given to the Taoist sage in ancient China.
2. J. Austin. Zen and the brain. The construction and dissolution of the self. *The Eastern Buddhist*. 1991; 24:69–97.
3. J. Austin. *Zen-Brain Reflections. Reviewing Recent Developments in Meditation and States of Consciousness*. Cambridge, MA. MIT Press, 2006.
4. J. Austin. Selfless insight-wisdom; A thalamic gateway. In *Measuring the Immeasurable; the Scientific Basis of Spirituality*. Boulder, CO. Sounds True, 2008; 211–230.
5. J. Austin. *Selfless Insight. Zen and the Meditative Transformations of Consciousness*. Cambridge, MA. MIT Press, 2009.
6. J. Austin. How does meditation train attention? *Insight Journal* 2009; 32:16–22. This is the publication of the Barre Center for

Buddhist Studies. (Also online at www.dharma.org/bcbs, under "publications.")

7. J. Austin. The thalamic gateway: How the meditative training of attention evolves toward selfless states of consciousness. Chapter 15 in B. Bruya (Ed.) *Effortless Attention; A New Perspective in the Cognitive Science of Attention and Action.* Cambridge, MA. MIT Press, 2010, 373–407.

8. J. Austin. Meditating selflessly. Chapter 22 in *Horizons in Buddhist Psychology,* vol. 2, M. Kwee (Ed.). Chagrin Falls, OH. Taos Institute, 2010; 417–431.

9. J. Austin. Consciousness evolves when the Self dissolves. *Journal of Consciousness Studies* 2000; 7:(11–12) 209–230.

10. J. Austin. *Zen-Brain Reflections,* 2006, pp. 187–226; 405–432. Most other cross-references to the earlier books will be in the form of brackets [ ] in the present text.

11. R. Buckner, J. Andrews-Hanna, and D. Schacter. The brain's default network: Anatomy, function, and relevance to disease. *Annals of the New York Academy of Science* 2008; 1124:1–38.

12. N. Farb, Z. Segal, H. Mayberg et al. Attending to the present: Mindfulness meditation reveals distinct neural modes of self-reference. *SCAN* 2007; 2:313–233.

13. D. Legrand and P. Ruby. What is self-specific? Theoretical investigation and critical review of neuroimaging results. *Psychology Review* 2009; 116(1):252–282. To appreciate the dual nature of the Self, it helps to undergo the *direct, first-person experience* of initially losing the *somatic* Self and then of losing the Self of the *psyche*. The two lived experiences, separate in time, confirm that each state is attributable to separable functional "compartments" in the brain. Ideally, a future critique of Self-referential correlations will have data available from very high resolution MEG techniques (not only the kinds of delayed data obtained from fMRI), plus a range of explicit tasks that will be designed and interpreted with extreme care [ZBR: 193–200]. At this future time, many thorny semantic issues that relate to "exclusivity" and "boundaries" can then be addressed using accurate measurements of the *volumes* and locations of the most appropriate modules of interest in individual subjects. This approach will be more accurate than scattergrams of single-peaks reported from groups of subjects during different experiments in different laboratories. For two recent examples of research that made excellent use of such volumes and boundaries, see A. Ioannides, G. Kostopoulos, L. Liu, and P. Fen-

wick. MEG identifies dorsal medial brain activations during sleep. *NeuroImage* 2009; 44:455–468; P. Downing, A. Wiggett, and M. Peelen. Functional magnetic resonance imaging investigation of overlapping lateral occipitotemporal activations using multi-voxel pattern analysis. *Journal of Neuroscience* 2007; 27:226–233.

14. "Horse sense" is still a sincere compliment. The phrase suggests the native virtues of a highly sophisticated animal, one who remembers the way to the nearest stream for a cool drink and the way back to the barn for bedding down.

Chapter 1   What Is Meditation? What Is Zen?

1. J. Austin. *Zen-Brain Reflections. Reviewing Recent Developments in Meditation and States of Consciousness.* Cambridge, MA. MIT Press, 2006, 6–11.

2. W. Shannon and C. Bochen (Eds.). *Thomas Merton. A Life in Letters.* New York. Harper-Collins, 2008, 362. Merton's letter to Suzuki was dated March 12, 1959.

3. S. Omori. *An Introduction to Zen Training. A Translation of Sanzen Nyumon.* Boston. Tuttle, 2001, 22. Omori Sogen and K. Terayama co-authored *Zen and the Art of Calligraphy* (Tr. J. Stevens). London. Routledge and Kegan Paul, 1978 [ZB:821; ZBR:433].

Chapter 2   Attentiveness and the Self

1. Mahasi Sayadaw. *Practical Insight Meditation.* Mindfulness Series 2. San Francisco. Unity Press, 1972. This is a 53-page discussion.

2. Bhikkhu Bodhi. *In the Buddha's Words. An Anthology of Discourses from the Pali Canon.* Boston. Wisdom, 2005, 281–290. A contemporary translation of the relevant section of this sutra is entitled "the four establishments of mindfulness."

3. In Sino-Japanese, *shin* is more accurately translated as heart-mind [ZB: 293–295].

4. T. Cleary. *Classics of Buddhism and Zen,* vol. 3. Boston. Shambala, 2001, 239–268.

5. T. Cleary, ibid., 410, 417.

6. T. Maezumi and B. Glassman. *On Zen Practice: Body, Breath, Mind.* Boston. Wisdom, 2002, 30–31.

7. Sheng-yen and D. Stevenson. *Hoofprint of the Ox. Principles of the Chan Buddhist Path as Taught by a Modern Chinese Master.* New York. Oxford University Press, 2001, 147.

8. Sheng-yen and Stevenson, ibid., 151.

9. Maezumi and Glassman, ibid., 61.

Chapter 3   Our Two Lateral Cortical Systems of Attention

1. Compare M. Corbetta, G. Patel, and G. Shulman. The reorienting system of the human brain: From environment to theory of mind. *Neuron* 2008; 58:306–324. The TPJ includes both the supramarginal gyrus and the adjacent superior temporal gyrus. Their ventral networking functions are sufficiently diverse to attend even to unanticipated stimuli that lack spatial dimensions.

2. M. Fox, M. Corbetta, J. Vincent, and M. Raichle. Spontaneous neuronal activity distinguishes human dorsal and ventral attention systems. *Proceedings of the National Academy of Sciences, U.S.A.* 2006; 103:10046–10051.

3. M. Koivisto, P. Kainulainen, and A. Revonsuo. The relationship between awareness and attention: Evidence from ERP responses. *Neuropsychologia* 2009; 47(13):2891–2899.

4. J. Brascamp, J. van Boxtel, T. Knapen, et al. A dissociation of attention and awareness in phase-sensitive but not phase-insensitive visual channels. *Journal of Cognitive Neuroscience* 2010; 22:2326–2344.

5. N. Farb, Z. Segal, H. Mayberg et al. Attending to the present: Mindfulness meditation reveals distinct neural modes of self-reference. *SCAN* 2007; 2:313–233. The twenty meditators (average age 46) completed the standard eight-week course of mindfulness-based stress reduction (MBSR). The control group was on a waiting list. Each group was assigned two tasks that required a different attentive focus. One task involved an "experiential focus." It required them to stay focused on their *present*-centered experience. The other (easier) task required them to engage in narrative ruminations related to Self-referential words. The inclusion of a "body scan" in the training process might be reflected in fMRI signals related to a region "along the supramarginal gyrus consistent with the secondary somato-sensory cortex." This region is far below the somatosensory *association* cortex of the superior parietal lobule, the region that helps integrate our sensory cortex into the body schema of a physical Self.

Chapter 4   Self/Other: Our Two Ways of Perceiving Reality

1. For discussion purposes, the two compartments are described separately. Of course, normally they are in constant functional communication, though anatomically divergent.

2. Even William James wrestled with this notion. Having regarded *con*sciousness as the kind of knowing that coincides with some

sense of Self, James then proposed the contrasting term: "sciousness." This word referred to the "pure and simple" variety of knowing that was un-branded by any underlying sense of Self. See: J. Bricklin, 2006. *Sciousness*, Guilford, CT. Eirini Press, 21–22; (ZBR:361–371). The present author uses the word "experiant" [ZB:34–35].

Chapter 5 Can a Psychic Sense of Self Be Cancelled?

1. D. Popa, A. Popescu, and D. Pare. Contrasting activity profile of two distributed cortical networks as a function of attentional demands. *Journal of Neuroscience* 2009; 29:1191–1201. This important study uses microelectrodes inside the brain to confirm that "task-off" regions (midline, fronto-parietal) show decreased field potentials and increased neuronal firing rates during attention. These findings are consistent with the possibility that "useful" coding and decoding can occur selectively in the brain as a result of intricate changes made in firing patterns that influence the degrees of synchronization versus desynchronization.

2. As the summary chapter at the end indicates, it can't be overemphasized how essential it is for future investigators to define which *intermediary* circuits and intricate neurochemical mechanisms cause activations and deactivations to shift in this seesaw manner on both sides of the brain. Reference 1 suggests the general nature of the problems involved.

3. Two facts are important qualifications on the oversimplications in the text. The first is that the cortical regions described are each heterogeneous, both histologically and physiologically. Clearly, their interactions (with each other and with the thalamus) are designed to serve more than a single function. The second is that fMRI imaging reveals the activations and deactivations to be only partial in degree [SI: 98–103]. The changes revealed in the BOLD signal amplitudes are slight—on the order of only 2% or so up or down from the resting "baseline." So the "hot spots" don't go on to "burn," as it were; neither do they become completely "cold." They merely become a *little* "warmer" or a *little* "cooler." However, the actual moment-by-moment content of the mental landscape of *the person inside* the scanner can be changing dramatically as a result of the kinds of neuronal changes described in reference 1. Such mental changes are in sharp contrast to the relatively minimal amplitude and frequency changes that are recorded by conventional fMRI imaging hardware and software.

These two considerations describe a substantial explanatory gap. They further strengthen the obvious case for accurate, *ongoing* first-person descriptions of the phenomena that occur during our states of consciousness. They also suggest how exceedingly selective and subtle are the physiological events that change the synchronies of our oscillations and the coherent connectivities of our networks. Major shifts have the potentials to enhance the flow of other-referential attentive processing while simultaneously reducing the maladaptive limbic input ("cancelling the noise") that has been overconditioning our Self-referential networks [SI: 114].

Elsewhere, two models of such "warmer" and "cooler" changes are envisioned (again in an oversimplified manner). See J. Austin. The thalamic gateway: How the meditative training of attention evolves toward selfless transformations of consciousness. In B. Bruya (Ed) *Effortless Attention. A New Perspective in the Cognitive Science of Attention and Action.* Cambridge, MA. MIT Press, 2010, 373–407. One visual model suggests the nature of such changes as they might occur during kensho (figure 15.5). The other hypothetical model addresses the neural basis for the changes during internal absorptions (figure 15.7).

4. J. Bricklin (Ed.) *Sciousness*. Guilford, CT, Eirini Press, 2006, 21–22.
5. P. Jokosovic and S. Todorovic. Isoflurane modulates neuronal excitability of the nucleus reticularis thalami in vitro. *Annals of the New York Academy of Sciences* 2010; 1199:36–42.

Chapter 6   Gradually Letting Go of the Self

1. Shodo Harada. *The Path to Bodhidharma. The Teachings of Shodo Harada-Roshi* (Ed. J. Lago) (Tr. T. Storandt). Boston. Kettle, 2000, 32.
2. D. Chadwick. *Zen is Right Here. Teaching Stories and Anecdotes of Shunryu Suzuki. Author of Zen Mind, Beginner's Mind.* Boston. Shambhala, 2007, 50.
3. B. Bruya (Ed.). *Effortless Attention. A New Perspective in the Cognitive Science of Attention and Action.* Cambridge, MA. MIT Press, 2010, 373–407
4. J. Austin. *Chase, Chance, and Creativity. The Lucky Art of Novelty.* Cambridge, MA. MIT Press, 2003, 185–189.
5. The contemporary scene includes many hunched-over, text-tranced subjects firmly in the grip of an electronic addiction, fingering their cell phone or BlackBerry. One antidote is to start letting go toward a different lifestyle—the kinds of heads-up, global attentiveness proposed in these pages.

6. G. Wulf, C. Shea, and R. Lewthwaite. Motor skill learning and performance: A review of influential factors. *Medical Education* 2010; 44:75–84.

Chapter 7 Two Complementary Categories of Meditation

1. The author prefers the term *receptive* because it has a well-established role in neurology. When *receptive* is used in the context of the normal language categories, it has the advantage of characterizing only the chiefly automatic, purely receptive language decoding functions associated with our temporal lobe. These pathways are activated before their processed messages relay farther forward into the "executive" language regions of the lower left frontal lobe. A further well-established distinction, with respect to language *disorders*, separates Wernicke's "receptive" aphasia (involving the temporal lobe) from Broca's "motor" aphasia (again involving dysfunction of the left lower frontal lobe).

    As the term *concentrative* is used in these pages, it describes the effortful ways we devote our top-down attention first to focus on two short-term working memory tasks (e.g., a visual focus, plus following each breath by counting numbers) and then to the supervisory role that keeps on actively *monitoring* how well we are still performing these same ongoing short-term tasks.

    We were actively supervised when we took tests back in grade school and high school. "Monitoring" then, as now, tends to imply that some visible person stays actively involved in a recognizable top-down, "watchdog" surveillance activity. Monitoring operations are set up to intervene actively in industry, not only in education. Monitoring is not limited to mere passive observation. Its intrusive stance is based on prior top-down decisions made to detect, stop, and correct aberrant events and behaviors.

    Therefore, if monitoring is to be a meaningful term introduced in the context of meditation, it seems most appropriate that we *begin* to apply it to some aspect of this more obvious, reasonably ordinary, quasi-voluntary preliminary effort to keep an eye on the way we try to perform our *ongoing*, top-down, *short-term* working memory tasks during concentrative meditation [SI: 39–41, table 5].

    Importantly, a more subtle level of overview operations also enters later during the course of more advanced, bottom-up attentive processing. This overview function seems more innate, implicit, and subconsciously exercised. Its capacities help identify gaps in our more abstract kinds of association processing. In this manner it helps large, complex problems to be resolved at preconscious levels. (This topic is discussed further in chapter 18.)

2. For a recent authoritative review, see A. Lutz, J. Dunne, and R. Davidson. Meditation and the neuroscience of consciousness: An introduction, in P. Zelazo, M. Moscovitch, and E. Thompson (Eds.) *Cambridge Handbook of Consciousness*. Cambridge, UK. Cambridge University Press, 2007, 499–544. The authors discuss the difficulties in using mere words to describe the complex factors that interact during meditation.

   A recent exemplary report from this team provides an explicit statement of the two different sets of instructions that were given to their experts and control subjects alike. (See D. Perlman, T. Salomons, R. Davidson, and A. Lutz. Differential effects on pain intensity and unpleasantness of two meditation practices. *Emotion* 2010; 10:65–71.) In this report, the "training for concentration" instruction was intended to encourage the subjects' focused (top-down) form of visual attention. It seemed designed to continually encourage them to *monitor* their ongoing attention on one small object. In contrast, the instructions to cultivate the other, totally "open" receptive state had an additional advantage in the context of this particular research. Why? Because it resembled the instructions for the second technique, previously termed "open presence" in the Tibetan Buddhist tradition. This particular open presence technique was one that their many expert meditators were already familiar with [SI: 113–117].

3. It is an age-old belief that "insight" meditation (when practiced for a long time) seems to help sponsor insights. Formal, multidisciplinary longitudinal studies are required for two reasons: (1) to prove this association scientifically and (2) to establish which particular components practiced under this rubric actually contribute to its mechanisms [SI: 123–188, 189–219]. It will be essential to assess the quality of receptive meditation and to have an accurate estimate of the number of minutes actually spent in such a receptive mode in order to truly understand both what "insight" meditation means for each subject, and how this first-person experience correlates with the subject's neuroimaging data. The same caveats apply to the focusing techniques used in concentrative meditation.

4. Formal, multidisciplinary longitudinal studies are also required to confirm that extended, accurately measured intervals of genu-

inely receptive meditation can serve to reduce (1) the activities of left hemispheric language regions and (2) the activities more narrowly linked with the well-defined Self-relational representations of the medial prefrontal cortex [ZB: 283–284].

5. D. Chadwick. *Zen Is Right Here. Teaching Stories and Anecdotes of Shunryu Suzuki, Author of Zen Mind, Beginner's Mind.* Boston, MA. Shambhala, 2007, 105.

6. J. Austin. Selfless insight-wisdom; A thalamic gateway. In *Measuring the Immeasurable; The Scientific Basis of Spirituality.* Louisville, CO. Sounds True 2008, 211–230.

7. J. Austin. *Zen and the Brain. Toward an Understanding of Meditation and Consciousness.* Cambridge, MA. MIT Press, 1998, 263–274; 591–592.

8. http://www.buddhistinformation.com/lecture_on_the_kalama_ sutra.htm. Here Bikkhu Bodi provides a comprehensive discussion of this sutra, originally part of Anguttara Nikaya, vol. I.

9. R. Aitken. *Miniatures of a Zen Master.* Berkeley, CA. Counterpoint, 2008, 23.

Chapter 8   Returning to the Natural World

1. J. Seaton (Ed.). *The Shambhala Anthologies, Chinese Poetry.* Boston. Shambhala, 2006, cf. 134.

2. The fortieth anniversary of Earth Day was celebrated on April 22, 2010. The next week a disastrous oil leak into the Gulf of Mexico reinforced the message.

3. R. Louv. *Last Child in the Woods: Saving our Children from Nature-Deficit Disorder.* Chapel Hill, NC. Workman Publishing, Algonquin Books, 2008.

4. S. Addis (Ed.). *Zen Sourcebook. Traditional Documents from China, Korea, and Japan.* Indianapolis, IN. Hackett, 2008, cf. 184. This poem was originally translated by W. S. Merwin and S. Shigematsu.

5. D. Chadwick. *Zen Is Right Here. Teaching Stories and Anecdotes of Shunryu Suzuki, Author of Zen Mind, Beginner's Mind.* Boston. Shambhala, 2007, 89.

6. S. Keen. *Sightings.* San Francisco. Chronicle, 2007.

7. J. Collester. Cézanne's legacy confronts high-speed rail in France. *Christian Science Monitor* June 14, 2009, 28.

8. S. Hawking and L. Mlodinow. *The Grand Design.* New York, Bantam, 2010, 156–166. After this universe began 13.7 billion years ago, it is postulated that the heavier elements in our bodies, including carbon, arose during the intense heat and other conditions

associated with the subsequent explosion of a supernova. In this sense, we and our planet are composed of stardust.

9. We tend to remember those "big" moons that rise in the early evening on successive nights around the fall equinox. The moon appears larger down near the horizon than at its zenith. These large moons have been called the "harvest moons." Coinciding with sunsets, the extra hours of illumination allow farmers to work later harvesting their crops. Several phenomena associated with moonlight enter into Zen at multiple levels [ZBR: 403–463].

Much of the illusion of harvest moons represents a complex processing bias. It arises in the back of the brain and favors an impression of image expansion (macropsia) rather than shrinkage (micropsia). It seems possible that this illusion (that objects are larger when they are lower down, yet still *above* the visual horizon) might "keep going," as it were. That is, one might ask the naive question: Could the illusion increase further (slightly) even if an object were to continue to descend *below* the person's usual visual horizon? If so, this capacity could be an advantage when we use our hands (e.g., while threading the eye of a fine needle) down in the lower levels of our peripersonal space.

Making due allowance for the influence of atmospheric refraction and other complicating factors, such a hypothesis would seem testable. For example, observers who were positioned at different higher and lower altitudes in space could measure the subjective versus the objective sizes of distant objects down near Earth at successively different angles of vision above and below their standard (straight ahead) visual horizon.

10. Analayo. *Satipatthana. The Direct Path to Realization*. Birmingham, England. Windhorse, 2003, 126. Our so-called civilized societies bring rising decibel levels and countless other complexities. These make it all the more imperative to provide every generation with an opportunity to learn how to meditate.

11. V. Lohr. Benefits of nature: What we are learning about why people respond to nature. *Journal of Physiological Anthropology* 2007; 26:83–85.

12. M. Berman, J. Jonides, and S. Kaplan. The cognitive benefits of interacting with nature. *Psychological Science* 2008; 12:1207–1212. This computerized task (like many others) requires the subject to focus attention on cues and targets placed in the center of vision. These tasks do not yet measure the full *global* extent of the brain's

attentional capacities to detect and react to unexpected targets that enter from the farther *periphery* of our vision. For example, the temporal crescent at the outer edge of each visual field is referable to a small zone in the anteromedial part of the opposite parieto-occipital sulcus. See F. Lepore. The preserved temporal crescent: the clinical implications of an "endangered" finding, *Neurology* 2001; 57:1918–1921.

Chapter 9   Settling Down and In

1. Shodo Harada-Roshi. *The Path to Bodhidharma, The Teachings of Shodo Harada-Roshi* (Ed. J. Lago) (Tr. T. Storandt). Boston. Tuttle, 2000, 133.

2. M. Raichle. Two views of brain function. *Trends in Cognitive Science* 2010; 14:180–190. This article is an up-to-date review of this important new field of research. To its discussion of metabolic considerations might be added the remarkable properties of nitric oxide (NO·) [SI: 260–261]. Nitric oxide can help reconcile several key events, such as: (1) The ordinary early increase in brain blood flow (vasodilation) that causes a transient increase in the supply of oxygen (in excess of demand) plus a corresponding decrease in deoxyhemoglobin. This combination could help explain why the BOLD fMRI signal briefly decreases. (2) The many dynamic variations that are likely to occur all along the meditative Path in neuronal firing rates and in various waveform patterns of synchrony and desynchrony. (3) The many changes affecting the functions of relevant deep nuclei (e.g., those of the striatum and of the acetylcholine nuclei in the pons), etc. Direct electrochemical measurements of NO· levels in animals could help clarify how relevant these and other potential NO· mechanisms are [ZBR: 279–290].

3. People's bodies and temperaments differ. People also change from one decade to the next with regard to what they become interested in and what they can tolerate. If you adopt a kneeling position, your open hands will rest closer to your hips. Eat less, for you will become sluggish after a full meal. One remedy for drowsiness is to open your eyes wider. If placing your thumb tips together helps you concentrate, try that. Keep exploring to find which postures and styles work best for you.

4. Zen refers to this lower midline abdominal region of the body as the *tanden* or *hara*. For beginners, it is not as easy to direct attention to as the nostrils. Its assets take time to appreciate.

5.   In the early morning (or when feeling sleepy later), splashing cold water on your face helps you feel more alert. Fresh sensory impulses from the face relay back through the large trigeminal nerve to stimulate your brainstem arousal mechanisms. There is another temporary way to stimulate this morning tide of arousal. It is to direct brisk, "sniffing" airflows back through your nostrils and sinuses. Try this by engaging in strong, quick, repetitive sniffing *in*-breaths—three sets of ten each. (I thank Emma Seppala for introducing me to this *early morning* "wake-up" yoga technique.) However, notice that any preliminary, warming-up, egocentric measures will benefit from being balanced by letting go into other-referential modes of attentiveness.

6.   Numbers and words are simply expedients. They're useful only temporarily, until bare attention settles down into being aware of each present *moment* . . . then into just *being* . . . then into *just this*. . . . The cry "shako!" (This!) is a word sometimes uttered in Japanese Zen as a way to point toward *just this* authentic reality. In Chinese, "jiu" on the in-breath, and "zhe" on the out-breath could serve as replacements for just this.

7.   J. Kabat-Zinn. *Wherever You Go, There You Are. Mindfulness Meditation in Daily Life*. New York. Hyperion, 1994, 112–115.

8.   G. Shulman, D. Pope, S. Astafiev et al. Right hemisphere dominance during spatial selective attention and target detection occurs outside the dorsal frontoparietal network. *Journal of Neuroscience* 2010; 30:3640–3651. Stimulus driven attention refers to other-referential attentive processing [SI: 57].

9.   R. Friedman and A. Elliot. The effect of arm crossing on persistence and performance. *European Journal of Social Psychology* 2008; 38:449–461. Debriefing reports showed that no students were aware that their arm posture had influenced their behavioral performance. For the purposes of the present discussion, a limitation on this excellent study is that both groups of subjects kept their fingers flexed and their hands closed. Moreover, achievement is not a goal to become attached to.

10.   *"What" is* their primary job description! The question and the answer are almost reminiscent of the old, classic routine of Abbott and Costello. Or of Master Ikkyu's response to the man who wanted to know what attention really means (said Ikkyu, "Attention means attention!") [SI: 3].

11.   Word labels have their uses early, but all words that reinforce the Self become subject to the law of diminishing returns.

Chapter 10 Looking Up and Out

Background I: Looking Up and Out

1. J. Sinclair. *The Rest Principle. A Neurophysiological Theory of Behavior.* Hillsdale, NJ. Erlbaum, 1980. An interval of rest can be the prelude to a spontaneous surge in activity.

2. J. Austin. Selfless insight-wisdom; A thalamic gateway. In *Measuring the Immeasurable,* Boulder, CO, Sounds True, 2008, 211–230. If pressed for a rationale for proposing gentle upward gaze as part of one's practice, it might initially be conceptualized at one level as a kind of "stretching exercise," implying that repeated practice might serve to set the stage for later spontaneous, involuntary, upward glances of greater amplitude. These casual glances might contribute to the rare convergence of coincidental mechanisms that become a trigger.

3. Often overlooked is the way that Siddhartha's six earlier years of rigorous spiritual training were the necessary prelude to his supreme awakening by this "morning star." In one sense, a triggering stimulus serves only as the "last straw" on an already overloaded (and sensitized) camel's back. With regard to Thoreau's comment that "all intelligences awake with the morning," the enlightenment of the Korean Master So Sahn (1520–1604) also coincided with his hearing the sound of a cock crowing.

4. A. Boduroglu, P. Shah, and R. Nisbett. Cultural differences in allocation of attention in visual information processing. *Journal of Cross-Cultural Psychology* 2009; 40(3):349–360. The subjects were students at the University of Michigan. The East Asian students were mostly from China. They showed a broader *peripheral* attentional focus than did Western students, and reacted more slowly to changes in the central region of the display screen. The subjects had a particular task: to detect changes in the spatial relationships of *colored* blocks. These peripheral and colored test conditions could enlist the fusiform gyrus in greater degrees of *allocentric* attentive processing.

5. V. Drago, P. Foster D. Webster et al. Lateral and vertical attentional biases in normal individuals. *International Journal of Neuroscience* 2007; 117:1415–1424.

6. P. Mamassian and R. Goutcher. Prior knowledge on the illumination position. *Cognition* 2001; 81(1):B1-B9.

7. Figure 4 shows mostly the *left* hemisphere. The discussion in this chapter refers to the comparable *right* ventral allocentric stream

over on the lower right side of the brain. The color phenomena described during short periods of morning meditation seem to depend on the entry of some light stimuli, through the gap between the eyelids, that go on to reach the brain. The phenomena during morning meditation did not develop in a completely dark room.

8. The author's earlier PET scan, performed during meditation [ZB: 281–283], was recently reviewed. It showed that the activity along the lower occipito → temporal pathway through the fusiform gyrus was much greater on the right side. Longitudinal studies are necessary to confirm this evidence that long-term meditation enhances more activity along the right allocentric pathway (**A**). In this regard, in 1974, a vividly colored Japanese maple leaf was hallucinated far up in the author's expanded left upper quadrant of internal vision during an early phase of a state of internal absorption. It too was referable to a sequence of (*early*) excitatory events involving the color complex region along the undersurface between the *right* temporal and occipital lobe [ZB: 482–487]. In 1982, all color was briefly lost *late* near the close of kensho. This achromatopsia is interpretable as a late, brief wave of secondary, rebound inhibition that blocked the functions of the lower color-sensitive pathways from entering consciousness [ZBR: 414–432].

9. P. Mamassian. Ambiguities and conventions in the perception of visual art. *Vision Research* 2008; 48(20):2143–2153. Major landscape scenes that included groups of people were sometimes assigned to the nonportrait category.

10. What determined this choice of three photographers? Only the chance location of their collected works in a friend's library. The three coffeetable books that happened to be consulted were Y. Karsh. *A Sixty-Year Retrospective*. Boston. Little, Brown, 1996; A. Kertesz. *Kertesz on Kertesz. A Self-Portrait*. New York. Abbeville Press, 1985; and A. Wolfe. *Migrations. Wildlife in Motion*. Hillsboro, OR. Beyond Words, 1994. Karsh chose to illuminate his portraits from the right (80 examples). They were illuminated less often from the back or bilaterally (52), and least so from the left (31). Landscapes by Kertesz were illuminated most often from the left (29 examples), less so from the back or bilaterally (27), and least so from the right (11). Wild animals depicted in migration by Wolfe were shown in arrangements that faced right (27 examples), left (23), or in mixtures of directions (44).

Background II: Zen References to Open-Eyes, "Open-Ears" Meditative Practices

11. Shodo Harada-Roshi. *The Path to Bodhidharma, The Teachings of Shodo Harada-Roshi.* (Ed. J. Lago) (Tr. T. Storand). Boston. Tuttle, 2000, 56. Harada-Roshi is the visiting abbot of the International One Drop Zen Association. His important chapter on zazen (pp. 49 to 67) describes the techniques of concentrative meditation and explains how they can evolve through stages into the one-pointedness of meditative absorption.

12. M. Moon. *The Living Road. A Meditation Sequence.* Newtown, New South Wales, Australia. Millennium, 1994, 33, 36. Milton Moon is a world-class potter who recently published an engaging illustrated narrative of his several personal experiences in Kyoto with Nanrei Kobori-Roshi and with the poet Harold Stewart. This book is *The Zen Master. The Potter and the Poet.* Stepney, South Australia. Axiom, 2006.

13. Sheng-yen. *Hoofprint of the Ox. Principles of the Chan Buddhist Path as Taught by a Modern Chinese Master.* New York, Oxford University Press, 2001, 139–158. The second image is Sheng-yen's summary of Hongchi's words. Sheng-yen discusses the various stages and techniques of "just sitting" that are part of (the Soto Zen style of) silent illumination practice (152–162).

Background III: Optional Positions of Attention and Gaze: Up, or Down

14. M. Moon. *The Living Road. A Meditation Sequence.* Newtown, New South Wales, Australia. Millennium, 1994, 82–83. The italics are in the original.

15. At our third interview in 1974, Kobori-Roshi had also demonstrated how to focus on a single leaf off *at a distance* out in the garden. His instruction was: "Look powerfully into that leaf, so that your vision goes directly into it. You must first learn to see into things and then through them." [ZB: 65]. No body scan entered into my Rinzai Zen instructions.

Background IV: Bodhidharma

16. The interested reader can view this statue at *picasa.google.com* by searching for "Bodhidharma Looking Up." When artists depict Bodhidharma as lacking both upper and lower eyelids, the result shows that an unusually wide circular zone of white sclera (normally hidden) surrounds his dark pupils. This artistic convention can (1) mimic some of the widening of the palpebral fissures

(retraction) seen in thyroid disease and (2) sometimes be carried further to suggest that Bodhidharma had an actual protrusion of the eyeballs (exophthalmos).

17. T. Terayama. *Zen Brushwork. Focusing the Mind with Calligraphy and Painting.* Tokyo. Kodansha International, 2003, 69. For contrast, the Bodhidharma by Miyamoto Musashi (1584–1645), a famous swordsman, depicts a fierce visage with eyes converged and looking down (p. 85). (It is easier for an observer to see the convergence of the eyes during near vision than the more subtle degrees of divergence that occur normally during far vision.) The Bodhidharma by the eccentric cave-dwelling hermit Fugai shows him looking left and slightly down with a concerned expression (p. 68).

18. S. Omori. *An Introduction to Zen Training.* A Translation of Sanzen Nyumon. Boston. Tuttle, 2001, x.

Background V: Relevant Examples from Tibetan Buddhism

19. *Mahamudra: The Moonlight: Quintessence of Mind and Meditation* (Tr. Lobsang Lhalungpa). Boston. Wisdom, 2006, 117. This is the second English edition of a sixteenth century text. The translation adds several comments (pp. 186–187). One is that open-eyed meditation surpasses all other meditation methods. Another is that looking downward can be a posture associated with meditative calming, whereas gazing straight ahead is (potentially) compatible with arriving at an indivisible union of great bliss with awareness of the void. The statement that meditators of the "Brahmanic order look upward" is not further clarified. If it were to refer to practices that some mystics direct up toward the sun, then such a technique of "sky gazing" could be hazardous to the retina.

20. A. Lutz, J. Dunne, and R. Davidson. Meditation and the neuroscience of consciousness: An introduction. In P. Zelaso, M. Moskovitch, and E. Thompson (Eds.) *Cambridge Handbook of Consciousness.* New York. Cambridge University Press, 2007, 499–544. This chapter notes that it is a delicate matter, even for an adept, to enter into the voluntary and discursive cultivation of such advanced refinements on the path toward a completely open receptivity. The term *open presence* is preferable to "open monitoring" whenever "monitoring" is used as an exclusionary term. "Monitoring" is a word at least at applicable to the short-term working memory, supervisory functions that one usually employ during concentrative meditation in an effort to sustain a top-down focus of attention.

21. Tulken Urgen. *Rainbow Painting*. Hong Kong. Rangjung Yeshe Publications, 1995, 63–64. The implicit nonduality of this state corresponds with the states of *kensho-satori* in Zen. In sky practice, the eyes are directed upward toward empty, cloudless space during an approach toward sustaining an open, empty mind.

22. Yongey Mingyur. Beyond Meditation. *Shambhala Sun*. 2010; 19:63–65, 90 (September).

23. T. Cleary. *Classics of Buddhism and Zen*, vol. 2. Boston. Shambala, 2001, 307. Shunyata is the Sanskrit term for emptiness. Mu in Japanese, Wu in Chinese.

Background VI: Gazing Up Involuntarily

24. M. Ricard. *Tibet. An Inner Journey*. New York. Thames and Hudson, 2006, 195. Shabkar was renowned for his composing and singing "The Flight of the Garuda." See K. Dowman. *The Flight of the Garuda. The Dzogchen Tradition of Tibetan Buddhism*. Boston. Wisdom, 2003.

25. Those fortunate to live and work in remote mountain valleys have ample opportunity to look up and out toward peaks high in the sky.

Chapter 11   Meanwhile, What Does "Being Mindful" Include?

1. J. Williams. Mindfulness and psychological process. *Emotion* 2010; 10:1–7.

2. L. Stryk and T. Ikemoto (Tr.). *Zen Poems of China and Japan. The Crane's Bill*. Garden City, NY. Anchor, 1973, xlix. Takuan was the abbot of Daitoku-ji from 1609 to 1638, a poet, calligrapher, and painter. D. T. Suzuki translates his famous letters on the tea ceremony (pp. 276–278) and on the art of the sword (pp. 166–168) in *Zen and Japanese Culture*. Princeton, NJ. Princeton University Press, 1970.

3. Thanissaro Bhikkhu. Mindfulness defined. Streetsmarts for the Path. *Insight Journal* 2008; 31:11–16.

4. Analayo. *Satipatthana. The Direct Path to Realization*. Birmingham, England. Windhorse, 2003, 44–66.

5. R. Davidson. Empirical explorations of mindfulness: Conceptual and methodical conundrums. *Emotion* 2010; 10:8–10.

6. Analayo, ibid, 44–66. Analayo suggests that by deploying some of sati's immediate softer affiliated attributes, we help filter, restrain, and select which particular kinds of information can enter through our sensory gateways. (Our thalamus and its reticular nucleus

constitute such a major gateway in consciousness.) Similar preliminary screening functions could help maintain a wholesome balance between our acute desires, fears, and other contending associations.

7. Analayo, ibid., 48.

8. Analayo, ibid., 57–58.

9. Analayo, ibid., 63. In the Theravada context, the noun *samadhi* is derived from the verb for "to collect together." It implies that the mind is composed or unified. Moreover, *right* concentration is assumed to begin with a crucial ethical premise: one's original motives are worthwhile and untainted. Sati implies that the observer is already alert and receptive and is enlivened by having diligently applied an ardent degree of concentration. Sati plays an obvious role in the calm abiding realms of *shamatha*. However, its qualities lose their natural breadth and become "mainly presence of mind" during the concentrated practices that lead to the deeper absorptions [ZB: 473 – 478; SI: 274–275]. See also R. Shankman, *The Experience of Samadhi. An In-depth Exploration of Buddhist Meditation*, 2008, Boston, Shambhala.

10. Analayo, ibid., 38.

11. The precise dynamic fMRI and bioelectric waveform correlates of all the neural constellations that accomplish our involuntary "re-mindfulness" have yet to be specified. Table 2 suggests that they will differ in their short-term and long-term properties. Moreover, their fast, fugitive nature (which contrasts with the sluggish lag time of fMRI) suggests that they might continue to be elusive unless magnetoencephalography (MEG) or some faster neuroimaging techniques were to be employed in the future. In the interim, chapters elsewhere consider the discussions of the kinds of immediative associative linkages correlated with the ordinary kinds of insight [SI: 123–188].

12. Patience (expressed in genuine tolerance) is one of the six virtues (paramitas) that a bodhisattva cultivates to perfection on the long-term Mahayana Buddhist Path of spiritual development.

13. C. Lewis, A. Baldassarre, G. Committeri et al. Learning sculpts the spontaneous activity of the resting brain. *Proceedings of the National Academy of Sciences, U.S.A.* 2009; 106:17558–17563. These normal subjects were trained not only to attend to an "inverted T" target in their left lower quadrant but also to ignore different "T" orientations in their three other visual quadrants. After only

several days they achieved 80% accuracy. (This took an average of 5,600 practice trials. Meditators who grow impatient with the essential role that repetition plays in their learning how to let go may wish to consider the implications of this number.) It will be important to determine in a future study whether meditating subjects, as opposed to their matched controls, become any more proficient after either concentrative meditation training per se, receptive meditation training per se, or a balanced combination of each style. In such future comparisons, it will be essential to arrive at an accurate accounting of the total number of minutes actually spent in each practice, the quality of attentiveness during each such practice interval, and precisely what is happening in the meditators' mental field while they are being studied. Accurate information about these crucial details is not yet present in the current meditation literature.

14. J. Allman, N. Tetreault, A. Hakeem et al. The von Economo neurons in frontoinsular and anterior cingulate cortex in great apes and humans. *Brain Structure and Function* 2010; 214:495–517. These bipolar cells might bring potentially intriguing involuntary influences to bear on our intuitions, awareness, emotions, and behavior. Their relative percentages are small (0.75–1.1%, or so), and how they influence their terminal sites has yet to be examined [ZB: 210–212].

Chapter 12   How Can Brain Research Help Us to Understand Mindful Meditation?

1. J. Greeson. Mindfulness research update. *Complementary Health Practitioners Review* 2009; 14:10–18.

2. K. Baerentsen, H. Stodkilde-Jorgensen, B. Sommerland et al. An investigation of the brain processes supporting meditation. *Cognitive Processing* 2010; 1:57–84. The fifty-two subjects represented three different schools of meditation: Zen, Yoga, and Tantric Tibetan Buddhism. The authors' candor extended to the caveat that "the findings in the present study are not consistent with those of other studies that, incidentally, are not mutually consistent either."

3. A. Lutz, H. Slagter, N. Rawlings, A. Francis, L. Greischar, and R. Davidson. Mental training enhances attentional stability: Neural and behavioral evidence. *Journal of Neuroscience* 2009; 29:13418–13427. Dichotic refers to the way the two ears receive different stimuli and how the subject monitors such differences. Future

studies would benefit from trained subjects who can keep an accurate, ongoing log of which kind of meditation or mind-wandering they were actually engaged in at a given moment of time.

4. J. Williams. Mindfulness and psychological processes. *Emotion* 2010; 10:1–7.

5. R. Davidson. Empirical explorations of mindfulness: Conceptual and methodological conundrums. *Emotion* 2010; 10:8–11.

6. J. Williams, ibid. The same attitude of friendly acknowledgment applies when other sensory, emotional, and cognitive events arise. They come; they go.

7. T. Horowitz, J. Wolfe, G. Alvarez et al. The speed of free will. *Quarterly Journal of Experimental Psychology (Colchester)* 2009; 62:2262–2288.

8. M. Cohen, S. van Gaal, K. Ridderinkhof et al. Unconscious errors enhance prefrontal-occipital oscillatory synchrony. *Frontiers of Human Neuroscience* 2009; 3: Article 54:1–11. Errors that are consciously recognized set off stronger adaptive control processes that last longer than those for nonconsciously recognized errors.

9. R. Berman and R. Wurtz. Functional identification of a pulvinar path from superior colliculus to cortical area MT. *Journal of Neuroscience* 2010; 30:6342–6354.

10. The Avatsamsaka Sutra describes a somewhat similar netlike web of interactivities as "Indra's net" [ZB: 499]. For a recent example of how individual nerve cells respond in the networks of attention, see T. Buschman and E. Miller. Top-down versus bottom-up control of attention in the prefrontal and posterior parietal cortices. *Science* 2007; 315(5820):1860–1862. The authors studied the correlates of attentive processing directly in 802 cortical nerve cells. They chose the particular times when their monkey subjects were focusing attention on two different kinds of visual tasks. In one task, the salient features of the target (its color and orientation) were very different from those of the four distracting stimuli. This kind of target is designed to "pop-out" and capture preattention instantly. The pulvinar is the main association nucleus of the thalamus and is likely to be involved in the early reactive sequences of such a bottom-up task [SI: 36–37].

11. M. Bar, K. Kassam, A. Ghuman et al. Top-down facilitation of visual recognition. *Proceedings of the National Academy of Sciences, U.S.A.* 2006; 103(2):449–454.

12. B.-K. Min. A thalamic reticular networking model of consciousness. *Theoretical Biology and Medical Modeling* 2010; 7:10 (This 18-page review has 127 references). The way our reticular nucleus gates important information from the basal ganglia and cerebellum merits much further study.

13. X. Yu, X-X Xu, S. He et al. Change detection by thalamic reticular neurons. *Nature Neuroscience* 2009; 12:1165–1171. Intrathalamic interactions will need to be decoded in future studies.

14. In humans, the reuniens extends for some 13 mm down past the hypothalamus into the upper midbrain. Intuitive messages rising from such lowly depths aren't yet attached to words.

15. Of course, other automatic responses also contribute to our many liabilities. This is where the restraints and renunciations of shila play an essential role in any programs of meditation.

16. A. Heller, T. Johnstone, A. Shackman et al. Reduced capacity to sustain positive emotion in major depression reflects diminished maintenance of fronto-striatal brain activation. *Proceedings of the National Academy of Sciences, U.S.A.* 2009; 106:22445–22450. This important behavioral and fMRI research was based on twenty-seven depressed patients. We await further multidisciplinary studies, both in normals and in long-term meditating subjects, that correlate the connectivities shared between various frontal regions and the ventral striatum.

17. The four periods (. . . .) in the two open spaces of figure 7 in *Selfless Insight*, p114, were chosen to emphasize that the brain's normal waveforms have yet to be measured and correlated precisely with each of kensho's selfless, first-person experiences as they unfold. [ZB: 536–539, 542–544; ZBR: 407–410].

Chapter 13 Why Go on a Retreat?

1. R. Herskowitz. Outward bound, diabetes and motivation: Experiential education in a wilderness setting. *Diabetic Medicine* 1990; 7:633–638. Using appropriate precautions, a strenuous program can be conducted safely even in diabetic patients. In the course of this program, the patients develop new insights, interrupt previous patterns of dysfunction, and increase their self-confidence and determination to "take charge" of their medical condition.

2. K. Erickson, R. Prakash, M. Voss et al. Aerobic fitness is associated with hippocampal volume in elderly humans. *Hippocampus* 2009; 19:1030–1039. These subjects were not meditators.

3. At home, by yourself (and with no obstructions on your path), after heel-first forward walking becomes habitual, you might try incorporating a fresh option: slowly walking backward. Allow the ball of the foot to contact the floor first, followed next by the heel. Stepping backward serves as a simple body practice for avoidance behaviors and restraint in general.

4. As a generalization, genetic and cultural factors may combine to make silence a somewhat more difficult task for women than men. See C. Brun, N. Lepore, E. Luders et al. Sex differences in brain structure in auditory and cingulate regions. *Neuroreport* 2009; 20:930–935.

5. Analayo. *Satipatthana. The Direct Path to Realization.* Birmingham, England. Windhorse, 2004, 250–265. No magic number, including "seven" is guaranteed, nor does any gradual or sudden progression toward realization unfold in a uniform stepwise manner. There is every reason to postulate that the Buddha would have continued to mature further in wisdom during his next 45 years as a teacher of others.

6. S. Omori. *An Introduction to Zen Training. A Translation of Sanzen Nyumon.* Boston, MA. Tuttle, 2001, 34.

7. D. Aeschbach, L. Sher, T. Postolache et al. A longer biological night in long sleepers than short sleepers. *Journal of Clinical Endocrinology and Metabolism* 2003; 88:26–30.

8. A. Ioannides, G. Kostopoulos, L. Liu and P. Fenwick. MEG identifies dorsal medial brain activations during sleep. *NeuroImage* 2009; 44:455–468.

9. M. Gujar, S. Yoo, P. Hu et al. The unresting resting brain: Sleep deprivation alters activity within the default-mode network. *J. Cognitive Neuroscience* 2010; 8:1637–1648. The twenty-eight male and female subjects averaged 22 years of age. The two regions chosen to represent the medial cortex were the dorsal anterior cingulate gyrus and the precuneus. The subjects had abstained from caffeine and consumed no alcohol for three days before the study period. During the previous week they had also maintained their usual average length of sleep and their same morning waking times. In preliminary studies, the subjects' number of hours of prior sleep correlated with how much fMRI activity was present in their dorsal anterior cingulate cortex.

10. J. Ong, S. Shapiro, and R. Manber. Mindfulness meditation and cognitive behavioral therapy for insomnia: A naturalistic 12-month follow-up. *Explore (NY)* 2009; 5:30–36.

Chapter 14 Preconditions for Fruitful Practice

1. D. Chadwick. *Zen Is Right Here. Teaching Stories and Anecdotes of Shunryu Suzuki. Author of Zen Mind, Beginner's Mind.* Boston. Shambhala, 2007, 46.

2. Bhikkhu Bodhi. *In the Buddha's Words: An Anthology of Discourses from the Pali Canon.* Boston. Wisdom, 2005, 322–323, abridged from the *Anguttara Nikaya* 8:2.

3. Joining a sangha is sound advice. Its members not only serve as your support group, they also invite you to make an obvious *other-relational* commitment in a community of fellow seekers. It turns out that subliminal priming provides many subtle effects that, by their influence on group dynamics, can help motivate you and your group to become more effective. See A. Dijksterhuis and H. Aarts. Goals, attention, and (un)consciousness. *Annual Review of Psychology* 2010; 61:467–490.

4. I. Grossmann, J. Na, M. Varnum et al. Reasoning about social conflicts improves into old age. *Proceedings of the National Academy of Sciences, U.S.A.* 2010; 16:7246–7250. The studies were based on 388 subjects in three age groups: 25–40, 41–59, and 60+ years.

5. T. Terayama. *Zen Brushwork. Focusing the Mind with Calligraphy and Painting.* Tokyo. Kodansha International, 2003, 25.

Chapter 15 Remaining Attentive Throughout the Day; Living Zen Practice

1. E. Hoffman. *The Wisdom of Maimonides. The Life and Writings of the Jewish Sage.* Boston. Trumpeter, 2008, 39–50. Moses ben-Maimon was a rabbi-physician (as was his father) during Spain's medieval Golden Age (the ninth to thirteenth centuries). He was well aware "of this screen that separates us from the Divine" (p. 73). He also wrote about meditation, saying that it "offers much help [in healing one's self], decreasing evil thoughts, sadness, and woes" (p. 92). [From chapter 3 of his writing on the "Preservation of Youth".]

2. S. Blackman. *Graceful Exits. How Great Beings Die.* New York. Weatherhill, 1997, 33.

3. S. Omori. *An Introduction to Zen Training.* A translation of Sanzen Nyumon. Boston. Tuttle, 2001, 98.

4. W. DeBary (Ed.). *The Buddhist Tradition in India, China, and Japan.* New York. Vintage Books, 1972.

5. Some long-term meditators reach a level and degree of "ever-present awareness" [ZBR: 184–187, 234–239; SI: 37–38, 288 note 1]. The evidence suggests that they have developed a more implicit

form of heightened ongoing awareness that is involuntary. In my own case, a similar phenomenon is manifest only rarely. It includes a greater memory for clear dreams and a greater alertness and clarity during the following day. Without having a nonmeditating twin, I can't be certain that my ordinary levels of awareness have been heightened on a regular basis [ZB: 295–298]. My tennis partners say that they rely on my reflexes, but this is anectdotal.

6. Red subconsciously evokes avoidance behavior. This can be demonstrated by psychological tests that assess performance in an achievement context. Does the habitual practice of gazing up repeatedly at a red traffic light subsequently influence a meditator's disciplined restraint in other subconscious ways? This remains to be critically examined. See A. Elliot, M. Maier, M. Binser et al. The effect of red on avoidance behavior in achievement contexts. *Personality and Social Psychology Bulletin* 2009; 35:365–375.

7. The other *paramitas* ("perfections") are disciplined restraint (*shila*), patience and tolerance (*kshanti*), resolutely applied energy (*virya*), meditation (*dhyana*), and insight-wisdom (*prajna*). Wright has formally analyzed these six ideal virtues: D. Wright. *The Six Perfections. Buddhism and the Cultivation of Character*. Oxford, England. Oxford University Press, 2009. He defines "character" as the portion of our overall identity that we define "by the choices that we ourselves make" (p. 7). As Olendzki points out, the roots of the word, *karma*, also hint at its *prospective* quality. Thus, the particular decisions we make that actualize our best intentions in daily life will shape the way our future character develops. See A. Olendzki, *Unlimiting Mind. The Radically Experiential Psychology of Buddhism*. 2010. Boston Wisdom, 145–147.

Chapter 16   Learning "Good" Habits Through Repetition: The Fruits of Meditative Practices

1. A. Graybiel. Habits, rituals, and the evaluative brain. *Annual Review of Neuroscience* 2008; 31:359–387.

2. S. Qin, M. Rijpkema, I. Tendolkar et al. Dissecting medial lobe contributions to item and associative memory formation. *Neuroimage* 2009; 46:874–881.

3. A. Graybiel, ibid., figure 5. We're learning that the sources of our habitual behaviors are almost as complex as are the pathways that drive our ordinary ruminating thoughts.

4. H. Yin, S. Mulcare, M. Hilario et al. Dynamic reorganization of striatal circuits during the acquisition and consolidation of a skill.

Nature Neuroscience 2009; 12:333–341. In place of their usual stable flooring, the mice learned to adapt to a rotating rod.

5. A. Karabanov, S. Cervenka, O. deManzano et al. Dopamine D2 receptor density in the limbic striatum is related to implicit but not explicit movement sequence learning. *Proceedings of the National Academy of Sciences, U.S.A.* 2010; 107:7574–7579. The humans developed serial motor sequences in response to a computer screen.

6. J. Kable and P. Glimcher. An "as soon as possible" effect in human inter-temporal decision making: Behavioral evidence and neural mechanisms. *Journal of Neurophysiology* 2010; 103:2513–2531.

7. S. Fleming, C. Thomas, and R. Dolan. Overcoming status quo bias in the human brain. *Proceedings of the National Academy of Sciences, U.S.A.* 2010; 107:6005–6009. The task requires the subjects to make fast visual decisions comparable to the "line calls" in a tennis match. In tennis, the line judge must *withhold* a response if the ball hits the line, but still signal "out!" when the ball lands outside the line.

8. G. Shulman, S. Astafiev, D. Franke et al. Interaction of stimulus-driven reorienting and expectation in ventral and dorsal frontoparietal and basal ganglia-cortical networks. *Journal of Neuroscience* 2009; 29:4392–4407.

9. G. Pagnoni and M. Cekic. Age effects on gray matter volume and attentional performance in Zen meditation. *Neurobiology of Aging* 2007; 10:1623–1627.

10. I. Schloegl. *The Zen Way*. London. Sheldon Press, 1977, 105.

Chapter 17   On the Everyday Practice of Gratitude

1. J. Austin. *Chase, Chance, and Creativity. The Lucky Art of Novelty*. Cambridge, MA, MIT Press, 2003, 152, 211–215.

2. [ZBR: 340] This figure 11 is entitled "Parallel universes, transformed by insight into oneness." At the top it illustrates the initial egocentric asymmetry: we perceive our Self-centered universe as larger than the allocentric universe. At the bottom, after the non-dual state of kensho, the figure shows that the other-relational frame of reference has now expanded to become the larger. Moreover, new porosities have opened up at the apparent boundaries between the two domains. During kensho, these structural changes transform the psyche. Thereafter, new porosities keep opening up during further long-term daily life practice. The result is a more balanced, fluid, flexible, interchange between our

versions of reality as we openly experience events in daily life [ZB: 21–22].

3. J. Austin, reference 1, ibid., 168–173.
4. *Oxford Dictionary of Humorous Quotations*, 4th ed. Oxford, England. Oxford University Press, 2009.
5. *The New Yorker Book of Dog Cartoons*. New York. Knopf, 1992.
6. *The New Yorker Book of Doctor* Cartoons*. New York. Knopf, 1993. The book informs the reader that this asterisk refers to the inclusion of psychiatrists.
7. M. Ricard. *Happiness. A Guide to Developing Life's Most Important Skill*. New York. Little, Brown, 2003. This is an important commentary by a major contributor to the field of neural Buddhism.
8. The Buddha's definition of happiness is in *Udana* 2.1.
9. Analayo. *Satipatthana. The Direct Path to Realization*. Birmingham, England. Windhorse, 2003, 233–242.
10. M. Moon. *The Living Road. A Meditation Sequence*. Newtown, New South Wales, Australia. Millenennium, 1994, 68–69.
11. R. Emmons and M. McCullough. Counting blessings versus burdens: An experimental investigation of gratitude and subjective well-being in daily life. *Journal of Personality and Social Psychology* 2003; 84:377–389.
12. J. Froh, W. Sefick, and R. Emmons. Counting blessings in early adolescents: An experimental study of gratitude and subjective well-being. *Journal of Scholarly Psychology* 2008; 46:213–233.
13. S. Koole, M. McCullough, J. Kuhl et al. Why religion's burdens are light: From religiosity to implicit self-regulation. *Personality and Social Psychology Review* 2010; 14:95–107.
14. A. Rapp, B. Wild, M. Erb et al. Trait cheerfulness modulates BOLD response in lateral cortical but not limbic brain areas—a pilot fMRI study. *Neuroscience Letters* 2008; 445:242–245. The inferior lobule is large, multitalented, and its supramarginal gyrus is usually included in the right TPJ [SI: 136, 146, 262]. High-resolution fMRI studies are required to assess the functions of any brain region in what is clearly a global, interactive context.

Chapter 18   Opening Up into Silent, Preconscious Processing

1. *Essays of Ralph Waldo Emerson*. New York. Harper and Row, 1951. Spiritual Laws, 99. The context of this sentence makes it clear that Emerson, ever the Unitarian preacher, was referring to divine guidance, and to the right-minded kind of "calling" that one might receive, wordlessly, from divine providence.

2. J. Austin. *Chase, Chance, and Creativity. The Lucky Art of Novelty.* Cambridge, MA. MIT Press, 2006, 159–168, 173–185.

3. Heard thoughts belong in a separate category described in table 3 as "conscious thought processing." Auditory hallucinations are not included in this discussion. They are considered elsewhere [ZB: 395–397].

4. A. Dijksterhuis and L. Nordgren. A theory of unconscious thought. *Perspectives on Psychological Science* 2006; 1:95–109. From a first-person perspective, each word that we hear ourselves think is a distinctive phenomenological event. We know when we're thinking because we "hear" our Self thinking it. We *recognize* this thought inside our conscious mental landscape. On the other hand, coded messages that are *non*verbal constitute the traffic patterns during our ordinary intervals of *pre*conscious processing. We transmit the gist of this information either silently, in the form of faint murmurings, or as coarse-grained vague visual images [SI: 28–29]. For this reason, table 3 prefers to limit the word *thought* to just this first category of *conscious* thought processing, not to the second category. In contrast, the table employs the word *processing* when referring to the second category simply to distinguish it from conscious word-thoughts. As discussed elsewhere, moments of thought-free awareness occur at several different times and ways along the meditative path [ZBR: 391–393]. Often their more intuitive associations are not attached to words. For example, conscience comprehends silently.

5. Elsewhere, the word *experiant* was introduced in order to convey the range of functions that we still go on experiencing when the conventional personal Self is absent from the field of consciousness [ZB: 34].

Chapter 19   Koan Practice at Deep Levels

1. J. Lori (Ed.). *Sitting with Koans. Essential Writings on the Practice of Zen Koan Introspection.* Boston. Wisdom, 2006.

2. T. Cleary. *No Barrier. Unlocking the Zen Koan.* New York. Bantam, 1993, xv, xvi.

3. T. Cleary. ibid., 7. The koan in this instance was "Mu."

4. L. Son and N. Kornell. The virtues of ignorance. *Behavioral Processes* 2010; 83:207–212. "No" has many uses in Zen. Not knowing implies remaining unbiased and open, not stupid. And no-mind, as Master Dahui said, means "a stable mind that doesn't get stirred up by situations and circumstances."

5. T. Cleary, ibid., 158–160.
6. J. Lori, ibid., 6.
7. J. Lori, ibid., 1. The dissolution of paradox cited by Lori points to a pivotal aspect of kensho [ZB: 678]. In this state, not only have all dualities been cut off from the inherent intellectual contradictions imposed by the koan, in the proposed model, a neural-Zen interpretation would suggest that the swift GABA sword cut of the reticular nucleus has also cancelled every other oscillation by the person's own networks of emotion that could give rise to a dissonant protest (chapters 5 and 6) [SI: 176–180].
8. J. Lori, ibid., 14. This is Ruth Sasaki's translation of the words of Chung-feng Ming-pen (1263–1323).
9. A. Dijksterhuis and H. Aarts. Goals, attention, and (un)consciousness. *Annual Review of Psychology* 2010; 61:476–477. The present author prefers to use the word *subconscious* to refer to the normal psychophysiological activities that occur below our threshold of consciousness. In neurology, the word *unconsciousness* usually has a pathological connotation.
10. A. Dijksterhuis and H. Aarts, ibid., 467–490.

Chapter 20   A Quickening Evoked by Re-Mindful Hearing

1. D. Suzuki. *Zen and Japanese Culture*. Princeton, NJ. Princeton University Press, 1970, 89–90. Masashige was a famed samurai swordsman. Before facing death in battle, he asked a Zen master, "How should I behave when I am about to die?" The master answered, "Cut off your dualism; let one sword stand serenely by itself against the sky!" Suzuki explains that the sword-slash metaphor of prajna stands for the full "force of intuitive or instinctual directness." This razor-sharp blade of intuitive-instinctual directness strikes with a much different visceral "feel" than do the messages that arrive from our higher intellectual levels. One reason is that prajna's insight-wisdom never splits into branches that could keep dividing *this* from *that*. No such academic hair-splitting blocks its swift passage. Instead, continues Suzuki, "like a knife, it severs joints at precisely the right point." This "one Sword Of Reality . . . never wears out after cutting up ever so many victims of selfishness." The next chapter has more to say about the keen, forceful, intuitive-instinctual directness of this Sword of Manjusuri.
2. J. Austin. *Chase, Chance and Creativity. The Lucky Art of Novelty*. Cambridge, MA. MIT Press, 2003, 132. I've long been aware that

my temporal lobes are connected with my hypothalamus. When musical sequences affect me profoundly, I usually experience the emotion of deep pleasure together with the hypothalamic triggering of gooseflesh that runs symmetrically from the back of my head down to the calves of my legs.

3. J. Austin, ibid., *Background I: coda*, xviii. Between the ages of 7 and 14, I spent many weeks each summer on my uncle Gibby's Ohio farm.

4. S. Harris, J. Kaplan, A. Curiel, S. Bookheimer, M. Iacoboni et al. The neural correlates of religious and non-religious belief. *Public Library of Science ONE* 2009; 4:e0007272.

5. J. Lutz, J. Brefczynski-Lewis, T. Johnstone et al. Regulation of the neural circuitry of emotions by compassion meditation: Effects of meditative expertise. *Public Library of Science ONE* 2008 March 26; 3:1897. Anatomical factors contribute to the effectiveness of an auditory trigger; our primary auditory cortex lies close to the superior temporal gyrus and the rest of the TPJ.

6. A. Blood and R. Zatorre. Intensely pleasurable responses to music correlate with activity in brain regions implicated in reward and emotion. *Proceedings of the National Academy of Sciences, U.S.A.* 2001; 98:11818–11823.

7. K. Henke. A model for memory systems based on processing modes rather than consciousness. *Nature Reviews Neuroscience* 2010; 11:523–532. The early involvement of medial temporal regions on the right side could correlate with the right-sided predominance of symptoms in the subject's descending pathways.

8. P. van den Hurk, B. Janssen, F. Giommi et al. Mindfulness meditation associated with alterations in bottom-up processing: psychophysiological evidence for reduced reactivity. *International Journal of Psychophysiology* 2010; 78:151–157.

9. G. Shulman, S. Astafiev, D. Franke et al. Interaction of stimulus-driven reorienting and expectation in ventral and dorsal frontoparietal and basal ganglia-cortical networks. *Journal of Neuroscience* 2009; 29:4392–4407. With regard to future studies of different techniques of meditation, earlier caveats cannot be repeated too often: researchers must design and interpret with extreme care *both* the "resting" control conditions *and* the tasks chosen for their imaging studies of selfhood and attention [ZBR: 197, 207].

10. Letters of Rainer Maria Rilke, 1910–1926, Volume 2. (Tr.) J. Greene and M. Herter, New York, Norton, 1969, 369. The setting was the

Isle of Capri. There, on February 25, 1907, his letter to his wife extolls, "breathing in-spring-sky" and "listening to the little bird voices." Absorbed in belonging within this natural atmosphere; he realizes that there's "no losing or missing anything." [See letters . . . ibid 1892–1910, volume 1, 1969, 262.]

Chapter 21   A Ripened Fruit of Practice: Cut Wide Open

1.   J. Austin. *Zen and the Brain, Toward an Understanding of Meditation and Consciousness.* Cambridge, MA. 1998, appendix B, 700–701. Seng-ts'an was the Third Ch'an Patriarch.

2.   Bhikkhu Bodhi. *In the Buddha's Words: An Anthology of Discourses from the Pali Canon.* Boston. Wisdom, 2005, 321, abridged from the *Majjhima Nikaya* 146; *Nandakovada Sutta*; III, 274–275.

3.   *Mahamudra: The Moonlight: Quintessence of Mind and Meditation* (Tr. Lobsang Lhalungpa). Boston. Wisdom, 2006, xxviii. When the previous edition of this book was first published in 1986, the title did not contain the words, "The Moonlight." No explanation is given for why "*The Moonlight*" has been added to this second edition. Even so, a striking white circle dominates the cover design of this 2006 edition. One and three-quarters of an inch in diameter, it "pops out" out of its dark blue background—the stark white image of a full moon. A more subdued moonlight reflection occurs on the cover of *Zen-Brain Reflections* (2006), where pages 405–463 consider the multiple literary and neurophysiological implications of moonlight.

4.   K. Kay, T. Naselaris, R. Prenger, and J. Gallant. Identifying natural images from human brain activity. *Nature* 2008; 452:352–355.

5.   Steriade and colleagues showed that a relevant stimulus prompts the fast frequency oscillations between thalamus and cortex to become "robustly coherent" for short periods of time [ZB: 613–617]. Such a reactive bioelectric response needs to be distinguished from the slower fluctuations of the fMRI patterned responses [SI: 114].

In Summary: A Sequence of Topics to Help Clarify the Mechanisms of Selfless Insight-Wisdom

1.   J. Austin. The meditative approach to awaken selfless insight-wisdom, in S. Schmidt and H. Walach (Eds.) *Neuroscience, Consciousness and Spirituality*. New York. Springer, 2012, in press.

Appendix A

1. Compare R. Bly. *The Soul is Here for Its Own Joy.* Hopewell, NJ. Ecco Press, 1995, 209. From "The Holy Longing."
2. D. Suzuki. *Studies in Zen.* New York. Delta, 1955, 40. Soyen Shaku is regarded as the "first modern Zen master of Japan." He represented Zen at the World Parliament of Religions in Chicago in 1893. D. T. Suzuki was among his lay students.
3. D. Suzuki, ibid., 38–44. In these pages, D. T. Suzuki translates several sermons given by Soyen Shaku during his later tour of the United States in 1905–1906. Soyen Shaku excludes eight varieties of "psychical aberrations" (including supernatural "powers") from the realization of the religious life. In addition, he notes that the Surangama Sutra mentions "fifty abnormal conditions of consciousness" which are to be avoided during authentic meditative practice.
4. It is of side interest to note that in their study of psychedelics, Masters and Houston also had exclusion criteria. Their criteria excluded most visual imagery, experiences of intense empathy, and experiences of "cosmological mysticism." They used these criteria, as do Zen masters, to validate which LSD "trip" experience was considered by them to be "authentically religious" [ZB: 426–436]. Multiple issues complicate the issue about the relationships between epileptic seizures and spiritual/mystical experiences. These issues are considered elsewhere [ZB: 349, 405–407; ZBR: 154, 423–425; SI: 264–266].
5. J-D. Degos, A. Bachoud-Levi, A. Ergis et al. Selective inability to point to extrapersonal targets after left posterior parietal lesions: An objectivization disorder? *Neurocase* 1997; 3:31–39.
6. L. Uddin, I. Molnar-Szakacs, E. Zaidel et al. rTMS to the right inferior parietal lobule disrupts self-other discrimination. *Social, Cognitive, and Affective Neuroscience* 2006; 1:65–71.
7. J. Taylor. *My Stroke of Insight. A Brain Scientist's Personal Journey.* New York. Viking, 2008. The quotations are from pages 60, 3.
8. C. Urgesi, S. Aglioti, M. Skrap et al. The spiritual brain: Selective cortical lesions modulate human self-transcendence. *Neuron* 2010; 65:309–319. The "self-transcendence" subscales index one's "creative self-forgetfulness, transpersonal identification, and spiritual acceptance."
9. J. Austin. *Zen and the Brain. Toward an Understanding of Meditation and Consciousness.* Cambridge, MA. MIT Press, 1998. Confusion

still exists about which phenomena occur during a state of kensho. The interested reader is referred to the eighteen major characteristics of the insight-wisdom of kensho cited on pages 542–544. The qualities of prajna (insight-wisdom) are discussed next, on pages 544–549. The discussions following this include the qualities of suchness (549–553), direct perception of the eternally perfect world (554–556), the dissolution of time (561–567), the death of fear (567–570), emptiness (570–572), and objective vision (573–578). The discussion of the levels and sequences of "nonattainment" is begun on pages 579–584. Insightful awakenings are also explored in ZBR: 327–464.

Source Notes

In the interests of this slender book, readers are spared attributions for many epigraphs, with these exceptions:

Part I. T. Cleary. *Classics of Buddhism and Zen*, vol. 3. Boston. Shambhala, 2001, 225. Yuan-wu Kequin (1063–1135) was a Ch'an Master in the Linchi (Rinzai) school of Zen, the author of the *Blue Cliff Record* of koans, and of numerous letters.

Part II. D. Chadwick. *Zen is Right Here. Teaching Stories and Anecdotes of Shunryu Suzuki, Author of Zen Mind, Beginner's Mind*. Boston. Shambhala, 2007, 107. This book is a rich source of wisdom from a pioneering Soto master who exemplified Zen in the United States.

Part III. (Cited in chapter 9) A. Braverman (Tr.). *Mud and Water. A Collection of Thoughts by the Zen Master Bassui*. San Francisco. Northpoint Press, 1989, xx.

Part IV. J. Cleary (Ed.) and T. Cleary (Tr.). *Zen Letters. Teachings of Yuanwu*. Boston. Shambhala, 1994, 55.

Part V. I. Schloegl. *The Zen Way*. London, Sheldon Press, 1977, 92.

Index

Aarts, H., 154, 155
Abdominal movements in breathing, 66, 68, 207n4
Absorptions, 9, 46, 188
  internal, 210n8
  superficial, 88–89
"Acceptance Practice," 139
Accumbens nucleus, 111, 135, 136
Acetylcholine, 138
Achievement test performance, arm positions affecting, 71, 208n9
Achromatopsia, 210n8
Activations, 173, 201n3
  in attention-on/Self-off reactions, 34
  in reciprocal cycle of slow spontaneous fluctuations, 34, 104
Addiction, electronic, 202n5(chap.6)
Adolescents, gratitude of, 144
Aerobic fitness, 118, 217n2
Afterimages, 19
Age-related changes, 128–129
  in putamen, 138
  in wisdom, 128
Aitken-Roshi, Robert, 51
Alertness
  in mindful introspection, 99
  in outdoor settings, 58
Allocentric processing, 171–172, 174
  and bare awareness, 83f
  clarity in, 49
  compared to egocentric processing, 24–25, 29

intuition in, 175
  in kensho and satori, 27
  in long-term meditation practice, 210n8
  objective nature of, 27
  perception of reality in, 25–28
  and psychic sense of self, 32f
  in receptive meditation, 72
  reciprocal seesaw relationship with egocentric processing, 6–7, 33–34, 35, 51, 104, 176
  shift from egocentric processing to, 29–30
  body language and gestures in, 40
  in peak experiences, 177
  reticular nucleus in, 36, 176
  slow cycle of spontaneous fluctuations in, 104
  triggering events in, 76–77
  as "southern" pathway, 27, 72–73, 174
  in what-type questions, 25, 27, 73
γ-Amino butyric acid (GABA), 35, 108
Amygdala, 107, 136
  in emotional responses, 161, 162
  in mindfulness-based meditative training, 20
Analayo, 96
Anesthesia, thalamus functions in, 36–37
Annica, 98
Anterior cingulate, 102
Approach behaviors, 169

Involuntary actions (*cont.*)
  and learning of habitual behaviors, 133–139
  in letting go, 39, 41
  upward and outward gaze in, 39, 57, 90–91
  ventral bottom-up attention in, 16, 18, 28, 175
Ioannides, A., 123
Isoflurane anesthesia, 37

James, William, 13, 36–37, 200–201n2
Joriki, 12
"Just sitting" practice, 84, 211n13
Just this, 8
  awareness in, 98, 183
  in breathing cycle, 67–69, 182
  in daily life practice, 132
  gratitude for, 180
"Just Walking," 119, 184

Kalama community, visit of Buddha to, 51
Karma, 218n7
Karuna, 93
Kato Kozan, Master, 129
Kenosis, 164–165
Kensho, 74, 76, 89, 163
  afterimages in, 19
  allocentric processing in, 27
  characteristics of, 227–228n9
  expansion of other-centered point of view in, 221–222n2
  insight in, 46–47
  in koan practice, 154, 224n7
  objectivity in, 160
  receptive and reactive mechanisms in, 50–51
  reticular nucleus in, 36
  triggering events in, 91, 109

Kindness, as habit, 142, 186
Koan practice, 150–155, 159, 186
  implicit learning in, 154
  incubation in, 151, 152, 186
  introspection in, 150, 151, 154
  kensho in, 154, 224n7
  not-knowing in, 152–153
  paradox in, 154, 188
  re-mindfulness in, 151
  summary (capping) phrase in, 151
Kobori-Roshi, Nanrei, 6, 8, 42, 50, 65, 82, 85, 144, 152, 164, 169, 175, 211n15
Kshanti, 220n7

Language, 47, 175–176
  cortical regions in, 19, 28, 175, 201n1
  receptive, 201n1
  and wordless clarity, 48–49
  and wordless insight, 19, 146
  and wordless letting go, 47–49
  and word-thoughts, 146, 223n4(chap.18)
Lateral cortical systems of attention, 13–20
Laughter, 143, 186
Learning
  declarative, 134
  in direct experiences, 100–102
  of habitual behaviors, 133–139
  implicit, 136, 155, 171
  in koan practice, 154
  in inverted T target experiment, 101–102, 214–215n13
  in meditative retreats, 116
  neuroplasticity of brain in, 100–101, 155
  procedural, 134, 138
  top-down attention in, 134

Letting go, 37–41, 175
  body language and gestures in,
    40–41
  bowing in, 39–40, 180
  breathing cycle in, 38, 180
  involuntary behaviors in, 39, 41
  lightening up in, 39, 180
  in no-thinking, 11–12
  in outdoor settings, 55–60
  in silent illumination practice,
    82–84
  simplification of lifestyle in, 9–
    10, 179
  wordless, 47–49
Lifestyle, simplification of, 9–10,
  179
Lightening up, 39, 180
Limbic system, 35, 108, 145
  in emotions, 35, 160, 176
Listening
  lowly, 145, 146, 147
  in outdoor settings, 57–58
Living Zen, 137, 138, 139, 145
Longitudinal fasciculus, superior, 150
Lutz, A., 104
Lutz, J., 161

Maezumi, Taizan, Zen Master, 3,
  11
Magnetic resonance imaging,
  functional (fMRI), 173
  activations and deactivations in,
    34, 201n3
  BOLD (blood oxygen level-
    dependent) signals in, 201n3,
    207n2
  in cheerfulness, 145
  in inverted T target experiment,
    101–102, 214–215n13
  in mindfulness-based medita-
    tive training, 20, 105, 200n5

in re-mindfulness, 214n11
research suggestions on, 167
in resting conditions, 31, 101
  and attention-on reaction, 33–
    34
in sleep deprivation, 123, 216n9
of subthalamic nucleus, 136
in top-down attention, 162
Magnetic stimulation, transcranial, 192
Magnetoencephalography
  (MEG)
  research suggestions on, 167
  in sleep studies, 123
  in visual processing, 107–108
Mahamudra, 88, 90, 212n19
Mahasi Sayadaw, 9
Mahayana Buddhism, 4
Maimonides, 130
Man-ch'uan, Master, 153
Manjusuri, sword of, 121
Masashige, Kusunoki, 156,
  222n1
Meditation
  analytical, 89
  body scan technique in, 41, 105
  bowing prior to, 39–40
  breathing in, 65–69
  compassion, 161, 225n5
  concentrative. *See* Concentrative
    meditation
  in daily life practice, 125–167,
    184–186
  downward gaze in, 65, 66, 75,
    76, 182
  experimentation with novel
    variations in, 51
  external attention in, 41, 180
  in indoor settings, 61–112, 182–
    183
  insight, 44, 204n3
  internal attention in, 41

Meditation (*cont.*)
  letting go of self in, 37–41
    wordless, 47–49
  little openings in, 156
  in long-term practice
    allocentric pathway activity in,
      210n8
    awareness in, 219–220n5
    balance in, 103, 170
    body language and gestures in,
      41
    bottom-up processing in,
      29–30, 162
    emotions in, 12
    incremental changes in, 29–30,
      111, 138, 180
    insight-wisdom in, 47
    nitric oxide-induced transfor-
      mations in, 138
    number of years in, 121, 218n5
    positive effects attributed to,
      110–111
    receptive and reactive mecha-
      nisms in, 50–51
    research on, 111
    selfless and wordless clarity in,
      49
    trait changes in, 4
  looking up and out during, 72,
    74–91
  with eyelids partially closed,
    75–76
  mindfulness-based, functional
    MRI in, 20, 105, 200n5
  mind-wandering thoughts in.
    See Mind-wandering thoughts
  no-thought, 11–12, 84, 146, 165
  with open-eyes and open-ears,
    81–84, 89, 212n19
  in outdoor settings, 53–60,
    181–182

  posture in. *See* Posture in
    meditation
  receptive. *See* Receptive
    meditation
  relaxed attentive state in, 65
  research suggestions on, 166–
    167, 188
  in retreats. *See* Retreats,
    meditative
  seated. *See* Seated meditation
  settling "down and in" as first
    step in, 65–66, 75, 182
  shifts of attention in, 44–45
  silent illumination practice in,
    82–84, 166, 211n13
  suggestions on, 179–188
  walking, 119, 184, 218n3
Memory
  associations in, 63–64, 92, 94
  engrams in, 63
  of meditative retreats, 12–13
  monitoring of, 94, 167
  overview functions, 92–93, 93t,
    94, 167
  and re-mindful quickening, 159
  retrieval of, 64, 95
  and *sati*, 94–96
  subconscious, 157
  temporal lobe lesions affecting,
    134
Mencius, 115
Meningiomas, 192–193
Merton, Thomas, 3
Meta-awareness, 44, 96
Metta, 142
Middle Way, 97, 183
Milton, John, 140
Mind, presence of, 93–94
  open, 89, 212n20
Mindfulness, 92–102
  and attention, 7–10

Sword of Manjusuri, 121
Synchronization, 201n2

Takuan (Soho), Zen Master, 92, 213n2
Tan, 5
Tanchu Terayama, 91
Task-positive and task-negative regions, 166–167
Taylor, Jill, 192
Tears
in auditory quickening, 157
of camel in response to music, 161
Temporal lobe
in auditory sense, 29
and frontal lobe pathways, 25, 149–150, 157, 175
and hypothalamus connection, 224–225n2
in memory, 134
in pattern recognition systems, 73
receptive language functions of, 201n1
Temporary states, 8, 10, 98
Temporo-parietal junction (TPJ)
circuit-breaker functions of, 105, 107, 161
global functional domain of, 70
link to intraparietal sulcus, 101
in Self/other judgments, 192
in ventral bottom-up attention, 17f, 18, 25, 174
Thalamus, 34–37, 50, 107
in anesthesia, 36–37
and basal ganglia connections, 109, 135
cortical connections of, 50, 106
oscillations in, 36, 50, 176, 226n5

dorsal nuclei of, 35, 176
and frontal lobe connections, 109
functions of, 108–109
geniculate nucleus of, medial, 109
in quickening response, 160–161
in interoceptive pathways, 20
limbic nuclei of, 35
pulvinar of, 106
in quickening response, 160–161
reticular nucleus of, 35, 37, 108, 176, 217n12
inhibitory role of, 108–109
in kensho, 36
reuniens nucleus of, 109, 217n14
in Self-referential activities, 176
in visual processing, 107
Theravada Buddhism, 142
Thoughts
conscious processing of, compared to preconscious processing, 147–150, 148t–149t, 223n4(chap.18)
mind-wandering. *See* Mind-wandering thoughts
no-thinking or no-thoughts, 11–12, 84, 146, 165
and thought-free awareness, 48, 223n4(chap.18)
word-thoughts, 146, 223n4(chap.18)
Tibetan Buddhism, 88–90
Top-down processes, 14f, 19, 28–29, 171
arm position in, 71
breath following in training of, 66–69
in concentrative meditation, 43